POETS OF THE
FIRST WORLD WAR

John Greening

GREENWICH EXCHANGE
LONDON

Greenwich Exchange, London

First published in Great Britain in 2004

Printed and bound by Q3 Digital/Litho, Loughborough
Tel: 01509 213456
Typesetting and layout by Albion Associates, London
Tel: 020 8852 4646
Cover design by December Publications, Belfast
Tel: 028 90286559

Cover: The Imperial War Museum image no. E(AUS) 1220

Greenwich Exchange Website: www.greenex.co.uk
ISBN 1-87155-79-X

Acknowledgements

Thanks to Neil Astley, Les Murray, Dennis O'Driscoll and Rennie Parker for pointing me in the direction of particular poems and publications; and to my colleague at Kimbolton School, Bill Skinner, for his enlightening conversation in the trenches. I am particularly grateful to my wife, Jane, for reading the typescript.

in memory of Clarence Melville Greening
1886-1964
(Royal Field Artillery)

OFFICERS OF THE 198ᵗʰ BATTERY

Was there really a Sergeant-Major Death
   in Grandpa's artillery regiment?
   Here's the name, falling in at the end
of a list of the Hundred and Ninety-Eighth

Battery's officers, marching in smooth,
   unironic, steady, cursive hand
   from General to Colonel to Adjutant
with nothing (except perhaps the faint wraith

of a recoil about its blue-black path)
   to make it more than just a name like Lieutenant
   Choked-on-mustard-gas or Captain Blown-into-
next-century. It has my grandfather's

brand of humour – branding the shed he bequeathed
   The Better 'Ole like a postcard from the Front,
   or sticking his scraped-out pipe-bowl under
my young nose so I have to fight to breathe.

                            John Greening
                         February 2004

Contents

Chronology

Chiefly of events on the Western and Literary Fronts

1914

Jan	Charles Sorley goes to study in Germany.
March	Anthology of Imagist poetry appears.
April	Hardy composes 'Channel Firing'.
May	Rosenberg to South Africa.
	Frost's *North of Boston* published.
June	Archduke Ferdinand assassinated.
	Brooke, Frost, Thomas, Abercrombie meet in 'The Golden Room' with Wilfrid Gibson.
July	Austria-Hungary declares war on Serbia.
August	Britain declares war on Germany 4th August.
	General mobilisation.
	Sorley imprisoned in Trier: he, Sassoon, McCrae, Hodgson, Graves, Brooke enlist.
	Thomas freelancing.
	Owen tutoring in France.
	BEF retreat from Mons.
	5ft 8in minimum height for recruits.
September	Battles of Marne and Aisne.
	First trenches dug.
	Western Front established.
	A.P. Herbert enlists.
	Blunden at Christ's Hospital.
	Binyon's 'For the Fallen' appears in *The Times*, 21st September.
	Dylan Thomas born.
October	1st Battle of Ypres.
	Kitchener calls for 300,000 volunteers.
	First Canadians arrive.
	Australians set sail.
	Turkey closes Dardanelles.
	5ft 5in minimum height for recruits.
	Blunden's poems published.
	Grenfell's battalion sent to France.
	Ledwidge enlists.

	Robert Nichols enlists in Royal Artillery.
	Vera Brittain at Oxford.
November	BEF originally of 1,000 down to 1 officer and 30 men.
	5ft 3in minimum height for recruits.
	Edward Thomas begins writing poetry.
	Brooke starts work on 'The Soldier'.
December	First air-raids on Berlin.
	Christmas truce on Western Front.
	Sorley writes 'Lost'.
	Edward Thomas completes 'Up in the Wind'.

1915

January	Germans use gas-shells.
	Zeppelin raids on Britain.
	First submarine attacks.
	David Jones enlists.
	Herbert Read commissioned to Yorkshire Regiment.
February	British forces advance in Mesopotamia.
	Submarine blockade of Britain.
	Russian retreat at Masuria.
	Gurney enlists.
	Rosenberg returns to London.
	Gibson publishes Brooke's 'The Soldier'.
	A.A. Milne joins Royal Warwickshires.
March	Festubert: gassing of own troops.
	Dardanelles attack.
	Some British successes at Neuve Chapelle.
	John McCrae at Neuve Chapelle.
	Binyon begs Elgar to set 'For the Fallen' to music.
April	Gallipoli landings.
	'2nd Ypres': first use of poison gas from cylinders.
	St George's Day (23rd): Brooke dies.
	29th: Grenfell writes 'Into Battle'.
May	*Lusitania* sunk.
	Battle of Aubers Ridge.
	Coalition Government.
	Owen in Britain.
	Grenfell dies.

	Graves and Sorley to France.
	Sassoon joins Royal Welch Fusiliers.
June	Zeppelin attacks on London.
	Russian front collapses.
	Vera Brittain enlists.
	Sorley composes 'Two Sonnets'.
	Owen returns to France: more tutoring.
July	Graves writes 'A Dead Boche'.
	Edward Thomas enlists in Artists' Rifles.
	Binyon spends two months as Red Cross Orderly.
August	Further disastrous action at Gallipoli: Ted Hughes' father is one of 17 to survive from his regiment.
	Blunden enlists in Sussex Regiment.
	Graves writes 'Nursery Memories'.
September	Loos Offensive. Kipling's son dies there.
	Graves' experience of Loos as recounted in *Goodbye to All That*.
	Owen in London: passed fit by Artists' Rifles.
October	Edith Cavell executed by Germans.
	Owen enlists.
	Rosenberg enlists in Bantam Battalion.
	Sorley killed at Loos.
November	Churchill resigns from Cabinet after Gallipoli disaster.
	Sassoon arrives in trenches, meets Graves.
	Edward Thomas promoted to map instructor.
	Owen posted to Thomas' camp; perhaps even taught by him.
December	Retreat from Gallipoli.
	Haig succeeds French as Commander in Chief.
	Gurney joins Gloucester Regiment.
	'In Flanders Fields' appears in *Punch*.
	Brooke's *1914 and Other Poems* appears: Gibson has share of royalties.
	1916
January	Conscription introduced for single men.
	Robert Bridges' anthology *The Spirit of Man*.
February	Verdun: 400,000 casualties on each side.

	Sassoon's battalion move to Somme: writes his first outspoken war poem.
	Owen in lodgings over Monro's Poetry Bookshop.
March	David Thomas dies despite Graves' attentions.
	Edward Thomas promoted to Corporal.
	Owen shows Harold Monro his poetry.
	Rosenberg transfers to Lancasters.
April	Easter Rising in Dublin.
	Ledwidge will later write his lament, 'Thomas McDonagh'.
May	Battle of Jutland.
	Conscription for married men.
	ANZACS arrive in France.
	Rosenberg sent to France.
	Gurney moves to Laventie sector.
	Sassoon's raid on Kiel Trench, Fricourt.
	Blunden to trenches at Festubert.
	Thomas writes: 'As the Team's Head-Brass' and 'No One Cares Less Than I'.
June	Kitchener drowned.
	Russian successes against Austro-Hungary.
	Sassoon awarded MC: sick leave for England.
	Owen commission to Manchester Regiment.
	Rosenberg arrives in trenches.
	Richard Aldington conscripted.
	Gurney in company of Welsh singers.
July	Somme offensive (1st July): 60,000 casualties on first day. Total British/French casualties: 620,000. German: 450,000.
	Lloyd George becomes War Secretary.
	Graves reported dead after Mametz Wood.
	Blunden: "the war had won and would go on winning".
	W.N. Hodgson killed on first day of Somme.
	Vera Brittain nurses her brother on Somme.
August	Blunden moves to Somme.
	Sassoon begins anti-war verse.
	Nichols invalided home: shellshock.

	Harvey POW in Germany.
	Gurney writes 'To His Love'.
September	Tanks first employed.
	Edward Thomas with Royal Artillery in London.
October	8th Battle of Isonzo – one of many 'sideshows'.
	French counter-attack at Verdun.
	Gurney moved to Somme.
	Thomas training in Wiltshire: completes 'Lights Out'.
November	Freezing mud ends British operations on Somme.
	'9th Isonzo'.
	Blunden awarded MC after assault on Thiepval.
	Thomas becomes Second Lieutenant.
December	Lloyd George becomes PM.
	French offensive on Meuse.
	Gibson on reading tour of USA.
	Rosenberg writes 'Break of Day in the Trenches'; his *Moses* published.
	Owen sent to France.
	Sorley's *Marlborough* appears.
	Gurney in a rest station.
	Thomas volunteers for overseas; sends poems for publication.
	Limericks appear in *The Dump*.
	Vera Brittain's mystical experience on anniversary of brother's death.

1917

January	Haig made Field Marshall.
	Edward Thomas to France.
	Owen arrives on Somme.
February	Bread rationing in Britain.
	Thomas to Arras.
	Ledwidge writes 'The Irish in Gallipoli'.
	Rosenberg joins Royal Engineers: wiring parties.
	Sassoon returns to France.
March	British forces take Baghdad.
	Romanov dynasty ends.

Germans retreat to new Hindenburg Line.
Thomas at Observation Post (Ronville).
Owen leaves Front for hospital.
Gurney writes 'Severn Meadows'.

April   USA declares war.
British push at Arras: Vimy Ridge captured.
160,000 casualties.
Mutiny in French army.
Gurney shot.
Sassoon wounded: to England.
Edward Thomas killed at observation post on 9th.
Owen rejoins battalion.
Sassoon writes 'The General'.

May   Mine under German front felt in 10 Downing Street.
'10th Isonzo'.
Draft in USA.
Gurney in reserve for 3rd Ypres.
Sassoon's *The Old Huntsman*.
Gas attack on Owen's platoon: has shellshock.
Eliot's *Prufrock* appears.

June   Messines Ridge.
Americans arrive in France.
Royal family renounce German name.
Owen sent to Craiglockhart Hospital.
Sassoon writes 'To Any Dead Officer'.

July   Passchendaele ('3rd Ypres'): 370,000 casualties.
Ledwidge killed.
Sassoon's Statement against the war: he is sent to
Craiglockhart.
Blunden gassed: later writes 'Third Ypres'.
Gibson returns from USA; eventually accepted for
Army Service Corps.

August   11th Isonzo.
Owen meets Sassoon in Craiglockhart.
Charles Causley born.

September   Gurney gassed: falls in love with VAD nurse.
Blunden gassed.
Rosenberg's last leave.

	Owen begins 'Anthem for Doomed Youth' in hospital.
October	Owen meets Graves. Writes 'Dulce Et Decorum Est'.
November	Russian Revolution.
	Separate peace with Germany.
	Cambrai: first major tank battle.
	Balfour declaration on Palestine.
	Rosenberg at Cambrai.
	Sassoon passed fit for service; meets Robert Nichols.
	Graves' *Fairies and Fusiliers*.
	Owen to Scarborough.
December	Jerusalem won from Turks.
	Gurney's *Severn & Somme*.
	Owen begins 'Exposure'.

1918

January	Wilson's 14 point peace proposal.
	Major Robert Gregory killed – Yeats' 'Irish Airman'.
	Edward Thomas' *Last Poems*.
	Owen attends Graves' wedding; begins writing 'Strange Meeting'.
February	Meat and butter rationing in Britain but convoys begin to ease effect of blockades.
	Sassoon's 'Suicide in the Trenches' appears.
	Pilot poet, Jeffrey Day, killed.
March	German Spring Offensive on Somme.
	150,000 British casualties but Germans over-reach themselves.
	Treaty of Brest-Litovsk.
	Moscow becomes Russian capital (further from Germany).
	Blunden leads wiring party under fire; posted home.
	Ivor Gurney conducts conversations with Beethoven.
	Owen at Ripon: final outpouring of poetry.
April	RAF founded.
	'Red Baron' is shot down.
	Germans attack British in Flanders.
	Haig's 'Backs to the Wall' message.
	Rosenberg killed (1st).

	Owen begins 'The Send-Off'.
May	Flu epidemic is killing 20 million in Europe, America, India.
	Owen writes 'Futility'.
June	Home Rule abolished: conscription in Ireland.
	Sassoon's *Counter-Attack* published.
	Gurney sends Marion Scott suicide note.
	Blunden marries.
	Owen rejoins Manchesters.
July	Execution of Tsar Nicholas and family.
	Last German offensive on Western Front.
	French counter-attack: 2nd Battle of Marne.
	Sassoon wounded.
August	Allied counter-attack with USA.
	8th August: "the black day of the German army".
	British advances.
	Sassoon sees Owen for the last time.
September	Germans retreat to Siegfried Line.
	Owen awarded MC.
October	German attempt to negotiate an armistice.
	Ludendorff is replaced.
	Gurney discharged.
November	Peace terms agreed.
	Kaiser flees to Netherlands.
	Armistice signed: 11th hour of 11th day of 11th month: rapturous reception at home, low-key on the Front.
	A further war becomes inevitable.
	Sassoon writes 'Reconciliation' and 'Memorial Tablet'.
	Graves writes 'Armistice Day, 1918'.
	Owen is killed one week before the Armistice.

Introduction

For many readers of this book, war will be something that happens elsewhere: in Iraq, Afghanistan, Kosovo or the Falklands. Nowadays, it is the concern of professional soldiers and only affects the average British family in so far as they react to what they find in daily newspapers, 24 hour television and on the internet. Even the lingering nuclear threat of "mutual assured destruction" and the continuing "war on terror" seem somehow distant and unreal compared with the latest films and computer games that preoccupy society. No major poets have emerged from the ranks of the army in recent years and no one really expects them to. The war poetry of today tends to focus on the distancing, numbing effect of television, on the moral No Man's Land of hi-tech combat, as in Jo Shapcott's *Phrase Book* (1992):

... This is my own front room

where I'm lost in the action, live from a war,
on screen. I am an Englishwoman, I don't understand you.
What's the matter? You are right. You are wrong.
Things are going well (badly). Am I disturbing you?

It is a very long time since bombs have fallen on England and even longer since there was volunteering and conscription on the scale seen during the First World War. Yet to understand the poetry of that period, we have to try and imagine it happening and then go on and imagine those same eager young men, often straight from school, being killed in their hundreds of thousands, in such numbers that death rather than survival was the expectation. Every household was affected. Everyone knew someone killed or missing. The entire able-bodied male population of a village or a community might be lost in a single attack. There is no need to visit Thiepval or the Menin Gate to realise this: the war memorials are still in place up and down the British Isles, in disused churchyards, at obscure road junctions, in the tiniest of hamlets. In many ways we have still not recovered from this trauma. Yet we have, I suspect, forgotten what it is like to enter a war expecting to lose thousands: recent conflicts have incurred more losses to 'friendly fire' and post-war guerilla tactics than to enemy action in the field. Indeed, there is little sense of a battlefield at all in modern warfare. Americans still have the memory of body bags returning from Vietnam, but even the scale of their casualties is dwarfed by those in the First World War. Verdun, The Somme, Ypres, however, happened almost a century ago now. Reading the poetry of the period is as much an act of imagination and recreation as reading the Romantics or the Elizabethans. 1914-1918 was another world, an old, class-ridden, imperialistic and ignorant world perhaps. Yet it is inextricably a part of our brave new reality, lodged at the very deepest level, traumatising us still.

For my generation, the First World War was *The Great War* – a grim black-and-white BBC television series watched by parents and grandparents in solemn silence every week back in the 1960s. This was a war that they never talked about, but which had obviously affected them even more profoundly than 1939-1945: it seemed important for them to see veterans speaking openly to the camera about what they had experienced. I only remember ranks of faceless uniformed men, all moving in silent jerky rhythms to portentous orchestral music, improbably huge guns cranked up, comical-looking 'tanks' toppling over barbed wire – and a great deal of mud. Richard Attenborough's film of Joan Littlewood's stage play *Oh What a Lovely War!* made more of an impression, showing in colour and with brilliantly choreographed satire how the people who survived it really felt about "The War to End Wars" after the initial bursts of "We don't want to lose you, but we think you ought to go ... " Their soldiers' songs made clear that they knew all too well the hypocrisy, the petty motives of the politicians, the incompetence of the generals, and the sheer futility of the various 'pushes' on the Western Front. They saw it most vividly that first Christmas when the opposing forces met up in No Man's Land for a chat and a friendly game of football.

What only gradually became apparent to a rather confused young teenager was that as well as such dark ironies, the procession of historical facts, the unmentionable horrors, bitter jokes and risqué songs, there was poetry. 'War Poetry' was, then as now, considered particularly suitable for the classroom, perhaps because so many of the poets went to the trenches straight from school. In the 1960s, it was chiefly Wilfred Owen and Siegfried Sassoon, with some Isaac Rosenberg. Ivor Gurney would hardly have been known. Blunden and Graves were appreciated for their prose memoirs. Did anyone think of Edward Thomas as much more than a nature poet? Or mention young Charles Sorley? Wilfrid Gibson had only just died but was already forgotten, Binyon still remembered only "at the going down of the sun". And women poets? Nobody had even thought to begin looking for them. But this was enough to convince one schoolboy of the power and originality of what he was reading. Here was all the absurdity and pathos and horror and black humour that he remembered from Attenborough's film. And, more remarkably, here were writers who had lived and died in the First War raising those very issues which were being debated on the streets of the late 20th century and filling the TV news bulletins. And all this was being conveyed through that most old-fashioned of media: poetry.

To appreciate the poems of 1914-1918 it is important to consider what poetry itself meant to many of the participants. The effect of Owen and Sassoon on readers at the time is hard to gauge in so thick-skinned and image-weary an age as ours, although it is worth recalling the outrage at Tony Harrison's poem of the Gulf War, 'A Cold Coming', when it appeared in the *Guardian* in March 1991. The feeling at the end of the First World War was that poetry was the only art form strong enough to contain the shocking new truths, even though nobody had ever used such imagery in verse before and many journals were unwilling to risk publishing it. The Russian Nobel Laureate, Joseph Brodsky, has compared the metres of a nation's poetry to sacred vessels bearing truth from generation to generation. Conveying the experience of trench warfare to posterity would be more like carrying nuclear fuel across high seas. For all the authority of Tony Harrison's work, it is hard to imagine his message about the futility of war being revered as Owen's has been. He was, after all, not fighting with the soldiers in the Gulf. The general feeling is, as

Auden said, that "poetry makes nothing happen", and particularly so now and in England. Poetry is not a language that comes naturally to educated readers any more – indeed, it hardly reaches them at all. But by the end of the Edwardian era, it was still considered the noblest of literary forms and to be (as Paul Fussell puts it) "near the centre of normal experience". Education involved much learning by heart, very often of patriotic, empire-building verses. Edward Marsh's handsome *Georgian Poetry* anthologies would be expected to sell 20,000 copies. The pentameter, which Ezra Pound made it his mission to break, was already imprinted on the minds of thousands of school-leavers becoming involved in the war. Modernists such as T.S. Eliot and David Jones would find their own way of expressing the fragmentation of society, but the best known war poems turn to the comfort of familiar metres, even if it is to show them being cracked and battered.

While one does not need to know much history to be affected by this poetry, a great deal of its interest (particularly in the lesser poems) comes from the military and biographical context. When we know why Passchendaele moved Blunden to write his greatest poem; or can locate precisely the ruined mausoleum where Gurney composed his only setting of his own verse; or trace the route 'Mad Jack' Sassoon took when he led his raid at Fricourt; or realise that Owen's experience on Redan Ridge inspired 'Exposure'; or contemplate the consequences of Graves missing the first day of the Somme; or wonder whether Edward Thomas really instructed Owen in map-reading at Hare Hall; or read of how one poet picked up the volume of verse left by another in his dugout; or begin to see how certain literary and political figures like Edward Marsh thread the lives of so many of the poets ... they all begin to seem like characters in some vast epic tragedy. Those in power smile benignly from a safe distance, saying with Sir Henry Newbolt, "Ah, it's a great age to live in" as the youth of England goes to its doom. To Newbolt and his kind, the Great War was an ordeal to test the mettle of the English people. Needless to say, Sir Henry, whose "light of life" encouraged many a public schoolboy to "Play up! Play up! and play the game", did not take part in the "game" himself.

I have tried to suggest some of the more intriguing parallels and juxtapositions and coincidences in the chronology which precedes this introduction, but readers wanting further details will find that Tonie and Valmai Holt's *Violets from Oversea* provides an excellent digest of military locations and literary connections, while Malcolm Brown's *The Imperial War Museum Book of the First World War* gives a useful summary of the progress of the war from jingoism and mobilisation in 1914 through to 1915, the "year of frustration", 1916, "a year of killing", 1917, "a year of pessimism and confusion" and 1918, "a year of disarray and of sudden, almost unexpected victory". However, since most of the poets concerned were only involved in France or Flanders, many of the 'sideshows' of the war are not strictly relevant and Brown's book on the Western Front is an equally valuable guide.

If there is one thing almost impossible to comprehend it is the sheer scale of the war in Europe: the British trenches, stretching 475 miles from Switzerland to the Channel, were the scene of unimaginable horror. In 1916, on one morning alone, 57,470 British soldiers fell, 20,000 of them never to rise. By the end of the 'Battle' of the Somme, there were at least one and a quarter million British and German casualties. Many of these were men who had never been soldiers before, and would not have had to fight if the professional army had not been decimated in the early weeks of the war. They in turn would have to be replaced by an even more rough and ready band of conscripts. This kind of deadlock and mass slaughter was quite new in warfare and there was no documented way of dealing with it. No one had anticipated what the invention of the machine gun would mean – such a thing did not exist in the long, hot summer of 1914. Nor was there any appreciation of what the onset of heavy rains might bring. A trench may offer protection from bullets, but it will also fill up with water. It will be a home for rats, rotting corpses, faeces, lice, disease, unexploded bombs, bodyparts and nightmares. It will be a place to stand knee-deep in mud and guts and wait for the end. To go through the motions of 'stand-to'. Occasionally to sleep. To long for decent food. To endure the continuous noise and stench and terror. To make intimate friends and see them obliterated before your eyes. And should you collapse under the strain of it all, either be bullied and humiliated for being a coward, or be shot for desertion. There were 6,000 miles of British trenches on the Western Front: reserve trenches, communication trenches, zigzagging their way to reduce the impact of shells, an Alice in Wonderland rabbit warren of madness, and opposite – the Germans in their equally insane *Looking Glass* world. In between the two sides was No Man's Land with its barbed wire and shell-holes and human remains, its deadly longstanding invitation to put your head over the parapet or go "over the top". Every man's dream was of a 'Blighty' wound, one just bad enough to send you home. Meanwhile, the only consolations were food parcels, singing, dreaming and camaraderie.

While the historical facts and the military accounts read in conjunction with the poems and the lives of the poets do add up to a fairly complete picture of the war, there is one book that reaches parts others don't. Paul Fussell's *The Great War and Modern Memory* is one of the essential accounts of how the First World War should be seen in the wider cultural context. It is Fussell who points out the disguising of mass graves with neatly regimented rows, the gradual reduction in the height requirement for new recruits, the importance of dawn and dusk in the life of the foot-soldier ("Dawn has never recovered from what the Great War did to it"), the influence of homosexuality, the apparently obvious but crucial point that the battlefields were absurdly close to home, how the Somme today still smells of rust, that "by 1914 it was possible for soldiers to be not merely literate but vigorously literary". Fussell is particularly illuminating on the power of the names. He quotes Wyndham Lewis on Passchendaele: "the very name with its suggestion of *splashiness* and of *passion* at once, was subtly appropriate". And he gives us a memorable selection of examples of what he calls the "feudal language" of poetry at the start of the war: a friend is a *comrade,* a horse is a *steed* or *charger*, the enemy is *the foe*, the dead are *the fallen* or *ashes* or *dust* and so on. The story of poetry in this war is the story of men trying to forge a new language in which the truth can be told. No one can fail to be moved by middle-aged Laurence Binyon's shocked plain-spokenness in his 'Fetching the Wounded', knowing how confidently he had proclaimed "proud thanksgiving" when he composed 'For the Fallen' in the smooth dialect of empire during the late summer of 1914.

As to what the Great War was all about – colonial ambition, personal rivalries, long-standing grudges or the inevitable working-out of some darker poison – there are enough books on the subject to occupy a lifetime. But these were not issues that preoccupied the soldier poets. Their concerns were more immediate: survival, naturally; how to be effective fighting men; and facing up to the fact of death. But also grappling with their personal beliefs, coming to terms with the incompetence of superiors, forging friendships, seeing those friendships shattered, learning to what depths of indignity and suffering a man can be brought. It is for this that we read the war poets still, rather than merely for their eyewitness accounts of the fighting. Jon Silkin reminds us in *Out of Battle* that "even the celebration of a 'war poet' creates unease". But as time passes it is inevitable that greater emphasis will fall on the 'poet' and less on the 'war'. The best of these were, after all, poets who chose to be soldiers, who went into battle as committed artists, determined to lay their humanity bare to the full experience, feeling that if all else failed them, the truth of poetry would not.

* * *

This *Student Guide* attempts to look afresh at some of the familiar names from 1914-1918 and to bring readers' attention, if only briefly, to some of the poets who are even now overlooked. I have been as generous with my quotations as copyright allows, and have provided reading lists so that titles can be followed up. These are by no means exhaustive and it is perfectly possible that there are small-press editions of the poets that have escaped my notice. The arrangement of the first eight poets I have chosen to discuss in detail is perhaps unusual: they are in order of age, so that those who lived longest and had the greatest opportunity to revise their work come last. I think that this highlights important developments and patterns in the writings, while reminding us that several of the key figures lived well into the age of *Oh What a Lovely War!* and even *Blackadder.* I have put another two poets together in one chapter because of certain connections between them, and because they were respectively the oldest and the youngest when they died.

In addition to a chapter on key poems of the war, which includes a discussion of women's poetry, work by some of those not actually in the trenches and a brief mention of foreign poets writing in English, there is also one dealing with contemporary poets who have been influenced by the First War. I was pleased to see that Andrew Motion, in his recent Faber anthology, *First World War Poems*, took precisely this line and included many of the poets I discuss. It may be that we are at last exorcising what Ted Hughes called our "national ghost", because a surprising number of living poets seem to be drawn to this period. But the fact remains that for many readers of this book the First World War will be a distant historical event. Even the potent imagery of poppies falling at the Royal Albert Hall, wreaths being laid at the Cenotaph and the Chelsea Pensioners marching down Whitehall no longer commands the attention of the nation in the way that it once did. Other video images of war and terror have displaced them. I hope that the following pages will remind a new generation of readers why we should not forget.

1

Wilfred Owen 1893-1918

The difficulty in writing about Wilfred Owen is that he has become more than a mere poet: just as Sylvia Plath's reputation was established as much by her suicide and the attentions of feminists as by her extraordinary poetry, so handsome young Wilfred Owen, killed with shocking irony just one week before the Armistice, is now the very face of war poetry, perhaps even of the First World War itself, and an icon of the Peace Movement. Our market-orientated society likes nothing more than a writer who has something to 'sell', who can be made to represent a recognisable brand, especially if there is a ready-made slogan: in this case, Owen's famous formulation, "the Poetry is in the Pity". As Dominic Hibberd points out at the end of his recent (and essential) biography, "for many years Wilfred was regarded as a fairly minor poet" but "the 1960s and Vietnam changed all that". The question whether there is enough of Owen that is not "fairly minor" to justify the kind of reputation he has acquired is one that we need to consider.

Certainly, Owen's work has divided the critics from the very start. Even Siegfried Sassoon, who was the single most important influence and undoubtedly knew the difference between poetry and propaganda, made some rather scathing remarks in private about the quality of Owen's work, while always recognising its potential. On the other hand, Robert Graves was bowled over by some of the later work and did not hesitate to call him "the real thing" and "a damned fine poet". W.B. Yeats famously refused to include any Owen in his *Oxford Book of Modern Verse* because he thought "passive suffering" an inappropriate theme for poetry; while later poets such as C.H. Sisson and Craig Raine have condemned Owen's work. Sisson takes issue with Owen's claim in his Preface, "Above all I am not concerned with Poetry", retorting waspishly, "Anyway, what right has a poet to say that he is not concerned with poetry? If his work is not that, it can only be some inferior form of literature." And Raine suggests that Owen "has read, quite uncritically, too much bad Keats and worse Shelley", that his language is "so frequently artificial and literary", that he "wishes to evoke rather than describe, and too much of that evocation takes the form of emotional blackmail, largely because Owen is insensitive to the possibilities of understatement". There are plenty of contrasting views one could quote, but even the greatest enthusiasts for Owen's poetry would agree that he is uneven. This is hardly surprising, given his youth. But if a poet's greatness can be measured by memorability, surely Owen's immortality is safe: in his later poems he wrote lines that lodge themselves in the head and are never to be forgotten.

The sonnet 'Anthem for Doomed Youth' comes relatively early in Owen's output, and it lays itself open to all manner of criticism, not least the poet Geoffrey Hill's that "he takes thirteen lines to retreat from the position maintained by [the first]" (quoted by Jon Silkin in *Out of Battle*), yet it works on a musical level, as an 'Anthem' should, in the way that Samuel Barber's *Adagio* works, by appealing directly to our emotions. Perhaps a better musical analogy would be Vaughan Williams, who in the slow movement of his *Pastoral* Symphony (1916-21) introduced a bugle "calling ... from sad shires". Craig Raine might say it is emotional blackmail, W.H. Auden might remind us that all bad art is "sincere", but the 'Anthem for Doomed Youth' is carried by its funeral music and the appropriateness of the analogies it draws between Edwardian rites of mourning and the casual death of the battlefield. This is why the Shakespearean "orisons" is acceptable: the entire poem is at such a pitch of formal intensity, the word does not strike us as an archaism or make us think of Hamlet. The sonnet's impact is not so much from the obvious onomatopoeic Lewis Gun effects as from the subtle placing of pauses and the metrical slow-march (with its spondee and gentle alliteration) of the final line. Admittedly, the battlefield squalor is barely even implied – that will come in the later poems – but the mood is captured, the offering is made.

Dating Owen's poems has always been a problem, but the Stallworthy edition, product of much fascinating work on watermarks and paper types, is as close as we are likely to come to a correct chronology. Stallworthy tells us that 'Anthem' was written at Craiglockhart Hospital in Edinburgh, where Owen was being treated for shellshock and where he first showed his poems to Siegfried Sassoon. Craiglockhart is the artistic heart of Owen's work and has been the focus for many later artistic enterprises, not least Pat Barker's popular *Regeneration* trilogy. But, as Dominic Hibberd has shown, Owen's life had already been more eventful than was generally acknowledged, and a good deal of his lively personal life has been suppressed by his family, eager to preserve the image of the wholesome hero of "pity".

Born on 18th March 1893 in Oswestry and brought up in Birkenhead, Wilfred Owen's early years were dominated by the Evangelical Church to which his family belonged. His close relationship with his mother (his letters to her read like love letters) is tied up with the religious atmosphere that pervaded the home and was only somewhat offset by the more practical influence of his stationmaster father. Wilfred was the eldest of four children and his skills with young people were put to good use when at 14 he became a pupil-teacher in Shrewsbury Technical School. Even at this age the language and secret world of poetry were beginning to attract him, but he had to move to Dunsden, near Reading, to work as a parish assistant in order to fund his higher education. His work with the poor proved a broadening experience, but so did his discovery on a bookstall of the poetry of Harold Monro, which advocated free love, Godlessness and the "beautiful Future" in place of Christianity. Preoccupied with sex and death (the two great themes of poetry, according to Yeats), struggling with illness, the effects of a cycling accident and the intensity of his friendship with a young boy, Vivian Rampton, Owen finally had to abandon Dunsden and its overbearing vicar, sacrificing all his hopes of any career but teaching in an elementary school.

In fact, despite a series of illnesses and failures, Owen fell on his feet: in September 1913 he applied to teach in a Berlitz School in Bordeaux, where in no time he was displaying a healthy freedom from puritanical restraints and family disapproval: wine drinking, cigarette smoking, going to the theatre and attending dances, appearing on stage in a music hall (in an act whose next booking would have been the Folies-Bergères!), he was even finding time to answer "the call of an Art". He lived fairly anonymously, spending Christmas on his own, but acquiring a good reputation as a private tutor. By July 1914, as the outbreak of war approached, the only battles on Owen's mind were how to fight off the attentions of a mother and daughter who had lured him to the Pyrenees, ostensibly for educational purposes. But the more significant encounter was with the French poet Laurent Tailhade, the controversial Decadent who (wrote Owen) "received me like a lover". He was to be a powerful influence on the young poet, giving him the confidence to hold on to his belief in his own genius even as the rest of the world was disintegrating.

Guilty, but assured of his purpose in life, Owen returned to England in May 1915 and was confronted by Kitchener's recruiting campaign. Another brief visit to a suffering France convinced him that he did "most intensely want to fight" and, once back in London, that October he joined the Artists' Rifles. Thirty-seven-year-old Edward Thomas had done the same, and it is quite possible that the elder poet instructed the younger in map-reading when they were both at Hare Hall. What is certain is that the CO at the camp, hoping to inspire his men, quoted the Latin lines from Horace, "Dulce Et Decorum Est Pro Patria Mori", little knowing with what bitterness they would soon be flung back. While lodging above Monro's Poetry Bookshop and showing some of his work to its proprietor, Owen soon negotiated a commission (not so easy if you were not from a public school) and joined the Manchester Regiment to train as an officer at Witley Camp, Surrey. Owen felt himself "marooned on a Crag of Superiority in an ocean of Soldiers", but he did not object to having his own servant and decent pay at last. By the time he was sent to France in December 1916, Owen was a brigade officer in charge of the 'firing point' at Fleetwood. He left with a "fine heroic feeling" even though England's mood had sobered since the Somme, which had all but annihilated the Manchester Regiment. Owen was part of the restocking process. The shock is palpable in his letters home, despite his jokey tone:

... we were let down gently into the real thing, mud. It has penetrated now into that sanctuary, my sleeping bag, and that holy of holies, my pyjamas. For I sleep on a stone floor, and the servant squashed mud on all my belongings; I suppose by way of baptism ... We eat and drink out of old tins, some of which show traces of ancient enamel. We are never dry, and never 'off duty'. On all the officers' faces there is a harassed look that I have never seen before, and which in England never will be seen – out of jails.

But this was nothing compared with what was to come. As they shifted between dugouts around Beaumont Hamel and Serre, Owen, suffering from trench foot and dysentery, was tempted to let himself sink into oblivion. But, determined to get his men safely through, anger began to replace humour in his letters. The contrast could not be more stark between the heroic expectations he had witnessed at home, the "glories" portrayed in the official Somme feature film, and the "seventh hell" troops were actually enduring. Some of the worst experiences would later spark his most powerful poems: sheltering in a vulnerable "old Boche dug out" (recently located by archaeologists) and seeing the sentry he had himself posted go blind ('The Sentry'), and having to wait and stare into the "terrible eyes" of his petrified men at about the time when (as he casually remarked to his mother) "I suppose, you would be going to church". 'Futility' and 'Exposure', too, were conceived when Owen and his men were marooned on Redan Ridge, the very hilltop where the Manchesters had been all but slaughtered two months previously: "The marvel is that we did not all die of cold ..." As if breaking into a species of free verse he would probably not even have known existed, he writes:

We were marooned on a frozen desert.
There is not a sign of life on the horizon and a thousand signs of death.
Not a blade of grass, not an insect; once or twice a day the shadow of a big hawk, scenting carrion.

In March 1917, Wilfred Owen somehow toppled into a cellar and concussion put him in hospital, but he was well enough to be in Line for a gas attack on 6th April, probably the one he remembered in 'Dulce Et Decorum Est' and to experience the 'Spring Offensive' which his last major poem describes. This culminated in his being blown into the air by a shell in Savy Wood and left half dead for some days surrounded by a fellow officer's remains in "various places round about". This, above all, precipitated Wilfred Owen's final collapse – into poetry, it might be added, for Dominic Hibberd reminds us that his shellshock "has to be recognised as an essential stage in his becoming the poet of the war".

It is important to remember how new and controversial the whole idea of 'shellshock' was: Owen must have had to endure some mutterings of the kind he uses in 'The Dead-Beat', and it is highly likely that one Colonel Dempster made some verbal accusation which left Owen feeling that he had let his men down. At any rate, after a brief stay at Gailly, Owen was sent to Craiglockhart where he received the latest psychiatric treatment, which involved reconnecting deracinated, alienated human beings with their natural environment, what Dr A Brock called "ergotherapy". The analogy he used (which was music to Owen's ears) was the myth of Antaeus, squeezed to death by the war-machine Hercules because he allowed himself to lose touch with the earth. Owen's 'neurasthenia' took the form of bad dreams, something which is apparent from the nightmare imagery in his poems, and there is no doubt that there was a therapeutic element in what he produced but that is probably true for every artist. The greater need was to show people at home what was really going on: those images Owen carried in his troubled mind, as it is said he carried in his pocket photographic images of wounds and corpses to wave at doubters on the Home Front, a fact which fascinated Ted Hughes.

Life at Craiglockhart was stimulating and enlightened, but of course the encounter with Sassoon was crucial. Reading Sassoon's poems he felt that here was someone who could speak truth without being diverted by beauty. "Nothing like his trench life sketches has ever been written", he gushed and the enthusiasm for the work soon turned into a passion for the man ("you have *fixed* my life") which Sassoon found embarrassing. He had been sent to Craiglockhart because he had just published his statement of protest against the war. He was committed to a poetry of "definite experience" as recommended by Edward Marsh, the politician and father of Georgianism. Sassoon also knew that poets had as much of a job to do as soldiers. He suggested changes to Owen's work even at this stage and his contributions to 'Anthem for Doomed Youth' (making it more overtly anti-war) have been well documented, but it was the new gates he opened for the young poet that made Owen's best-known poems possible, incorporating (as Hibberd puts it) "actual incident, direct speech and army slang". In October 1917, Owen probably drafted 'Dulce Et Decorum Est ', 'Disabled', 'Insensibility', 'The Sentry' and polished others in the light of his new aesthetic understanding. Owen would never lose his Keatsian gestures and he was reading his volume of Swinburne up to his death, but here was the breath of modern life, the splash of contemporary colour that his verse needed.

What Sassoon felt Owen the man needed is another matter. What exactly was he implying when he gave him a £10 note, the address of Robert Ross, a prominent 'Uranian' (Oscar Wilde's first lover) and wrote: "Why *shouldn't* you enjoy your leave?"? Owen was offended, but Ross's good word was a way into literary London and tea with H.G.Wells and Arnold Bennett, but more particularly the Sitwells and Charles Scott Moncrieff, who promptly fell in love with him and may even have seduced him. Owen had already been introduced to Robert Graves and would later attend his wedding (though Graves describes him as a "weakling", uneasy about his "passive homosexual streak") but by November 1917 Owen was recalled to his unit in Scarborough, where he wrote 'Exposure' and 'The Parable of the Old Man and the Young'. Then, in March, to Ripon, where he rented a cottage in Borrage Lane and, in a windowless attic room, set out to find his true voice: 'The Send-Off', 'Futility' 'Strange Meeting', 'Mental Cases' ... As Dominic Hibberd puts it, "in all the history of English poetry, there can have been few braver, more extraordinary undertakings than his at Ripon".

After a final family reunion in April and more time at Scarborough, Owen was passed fit for service in June and found himself again "at work – teaching Christ to lift his crown by numbers", but was not sent overseas until 31st August because of a scare over an apparent heart murmur. Uncomfortable with junior officers who perhaps knew something of his background, Owen kept aloof in Étaples and Amiens, although he grew inordinately fond of his servant, Jones. The Germans had retreated to the Hindenburg Line and the task facing

Owen's men was to break the reserve system. Owen the anti-war poet behaved heroically as the Germans counter-attacked, holding off their advance single-handedly with a Lewis Gun, for which he was awarded the MC. But even Owen could not stack the odds in his own favour when it came to the attack on the Oise-Sambre Canal on the morning of 4th November. News of his death reached his family on the day the Armistice was signed.

Owen's reputation is saved for posterity because of those intense sessions in Ripon, Scarborough and Craiglockhart. 'Futility' is a poem that eschews the romantic as much as it does the anti-romantic (none of Owen's obsession with wounds and bleeding here) and can make an astonishing impact even at a first reading. It does not rely on the hammer-blow trochaics of 'Mental Cases', also written in May 1918, yet it does use that metre in its firm but kindly opening suggestion: "Move him into the sun". If the battlefield is "like the face of the moon, chaotic, crater-ridden, uninhabitable, awful, the abode of madness" (as one of his letters puts it), the sun must be the opposite. It represents home and comfort and hope and renewal. We know little about the victim, afflicted with "this snow" but the suggestion is that he was a farm-worker, for whom the seasons were crucial. As Jon Silkin explains at length in his study of the war poets, nature was a vital force in their work and nowhere more so than in Owen, although he is not a 'nature poet' as Edward Thomas or Blunden or even Sassoon was. The symmetry of 'Futility' is particularly effective. Having been asked to "Move him" in the first line of the first stanza, the first line of the second asks us instead to "Think". There is a note of desperation, a desperate searching for a solution that thinking cannot provide, only faith can – and Owen appears to have lost that. The sun is the only god in this poem and he is stranded impotently in the first stanza. The stuttering uncertainty of "Woke, once, the clays of a cold star" suggests something trying to be born, but perhaps only Ted Hughes' Crow. Just as Crow will laugh at God even as he survives the wasteland and proves himself "stronger than death", so the poet here sees the sunbeams as "fatuous", a wonderfully un-Keatsian choice of adjective, whose f-sound and vaguely insulting first syllable are redolent of trench-language – and far more than when Owen is deliberately trying to use soldier-speak. The poem ends with an unanswerable question, hurled out in laughing despair.

8

The "kind old sun" will go on shining, but it has suddenly come to seem as ineffectual as Sassoon's beaming General.

'The Send-Off' is another product of Ripon and owes something to the moorland surroundings, but also perhaps to Owen's Dunsden days, where there was a 150-foot deep well on the green. It is one of Owen's most advanced and fluid creations. He has shaken off the Victorian trappings, while keeping his own pure form. Although the style proves that there is (as Yeats decided) "more enterprise in walking naked", the poem feels densely written, emotions of shame, guilt, disillusionment seething in those "close darkening lanes". The men "sang their way" rather than just singing for the joy of it: their way was prepared for them – the image conjured is of sand disappearing down an hourglass, and the lineation emphasises this. There is a continuous tension between what beauty or heroism urges the poet to say, and what he knows to be true. The short line tugs at the long line: "Their breasts were stuck all white with wreath and spray/ As men's are, dead." Owen has by now discovered pararhyme (half rhyme/slant rhyme/eye rhyme) but feels no need for any such effects here. The full rhymes of "way" and "gay", then "spray", play sardonically against "siding-shed" and "dead" with the pointedness that Siegfried Sassoon taught him, although this goes beyond the derivative style Owen adopts in earlier poems. 'The Send-Off' ends in a daze, with an England where the wells are still pure, but where there are hardly any men to drink from them.

Of the other war poems, several stand out. 'The Sentry' is perhaps not as well known as 'Dulce Et Decorum Est ', but it is similar in construction, with the sudden introduction of direct speech halfway through, the touch of the grotesque ("Eyeballs, huge-bulged like squids'"), the emphasis on pity and the ironic last line. 'Dulce Et ...' is too much a part of most readers' mental furniture to need much further commentary. It too uses full rhyme to devastating effect in its final lines, but the melodrama of the gassing, vivid as reportage, weakens the poem, as do the fragments of Owen's Swinburnian nightmares ("a devil's sick of sin"). Yet no one could deny the cumulative power of the final single sentence or the dramatic impact a live reading of the poem can make, the sudden interjection of that shouted warning reminding us that Wilfred Owen was no mean actor and a great fan of all things theatrical. In the end, 'Dulce Et Decorum

Est' is a poem that tries too hard, something which could not be said of the effectively understated 'Futility' and 'The Send-Off', yet which might well apply to several other famous poems, even to 'Strange Meeting'.

For all its originality in the use of pararhyme, 'Strange Meeting' is a poem that this reader at least finds himself putting up with for its ideas, its moving individual lines and for its glorious epilogue. Like many of Owen's longer pieces, it over-reaches itself into the realms of abstraction and falls back on antique diction ("cess of war") donning the Victorian embroidered coat ("grieves richlier"), even letting those infectious half-rhymes take control of the poem from "tigress" to "progress", from "mystery" to "mastery" in a punning way that seems inappropriate to its lofty, Dantean tone. 'Insensibility' is much more effective in its use of pararhyme, is more original metrically and makes fewer concessions to romanticism. "Happy are men who yet before they are killed/Can let their veins run cold ...". When the rhymes don't quite click shut, it leaves an uncomfortable feeling of incompleteness, of something not quite right, like a discord in music. Unlike 'Strange Meeting', 'Insensibility' does not employ direct speech, yet the poem itself is much more in touch with the spoken idiom: "The front line withers ... They have enough to carry with ammunition ... His days are worth forgetting more than not ..."

It certainly makes more sense to place 'Exposure' (as Stallworthy does) among those poems written at Scarborough rather than early in 1916, which is where it used to appear. Even if it does rather lose its way, this is one of Owen's major achievements, not least for the commemorating of his men's grim ordeal on Redan Ridge. The extravagance of the pararhyme suits this kind of exterior 'action' poem rather better than it does the marbled columns of 'Strange Meeting'. The half-smile that always accompanies half-rhyme matches the gallows humour of the Front as the "sentries whisper, curious, nervous". Few other war poems capture the feeling of helpless isolation, the dawning of the madness of it all, as the opening stanzas of 'Exposure', and the relentless repetition of "But nothing happens" is a bold experiment (Owen does not often use a refrain) that succeeds admirably. The problem is, of course, where to take a poem about nothing happening: into abstraction is Owen's answer, sadly. But not so deeply in that the poem is not able to rally, regroup, and return us to the definite realities of the cold. Ironically, there is less 'exposure' in the language of this poem than in some of the shorter ones; but it will always be admired and remembered.

The best of the sonnets, along with 'The Next War', is actually a little less and a little more than a sonnet: 'The Parable of the Old Man and the Young' tells in 14 lines the story of Abraham and Isaac, but adds a vicious extra couplet: "But the old man would not so, but slew his son,/And half the seed of Europe one by one." This 'parable', like several of the poems discussed here, was memorably set to music by Benjamin Britten in his *War Requiem*, juxtaposing Owen's words sung by German or British singers with the Latin mass. Britten's pacifistic devotion to Owen's work contributed considerably to public interest in the work after the Second World War. That interest is unlikely to wane as each new generation finds its representative Owen poem: perhaps it will be 'Spring Offensive', Owen's last completed work, which sounds like the creation of a man who has found a voice and knows at last what he can do with it, knows too that this is not necessarily his only voice. He can do without Keats, but for the purposes of 'Spring Offensive' Keats remains murmurously buzzing around him, as does his taste for the theatrical alliteration ("Fearfully flashed") the sentimental gesture ("clutched and clung") the archaic word ("begird"), the religious imagery ("set sudden cups/In thousands for their blood"). But this is the voice of a poet who fought his way to find himself, his individuality, to control and channel and tame and shape the images that terrorised him, to free himself from the clutches of false idols and public lies and hypocrisy. That he achieved so much by the age of 25 is remarkable. He would be amazed to find how "Little Owen" has himself been made into an idol.

Further Reading

Owen:
The Poems of Wilfred Owen, (ed. Stallworthy, Chatto & Windus, 1990)
Selected Letters, (ed. J. Bell, OUP, 1998)
                          * * *
Hibberd, Dominic, *Wilfred Owen* (Weidenfeld & Nicholson, 2002)
Raine, Craig, essay in *Haydn and the Valve-Trumpet* (Faber, 1990)

Silkin, Jon, *Out of Battle* (Routledge and Kegan Paul, 1972)
Stallworthy, Jon, *Wilfred Owen: A Biography* (1974)

2

Isaac Rosenberg 1890-1918

By the time Isaac Rosenberg volunteered, in October 1915, the mood of jingoism had quietened, the celebrants of war as a heroic mission in which "gallant warriors" with "sword" and "steed" would "assail" and "vanquish" were already made to have second thoughts with the death of Rupert Brooke. Etonian Julian Grenfell and Marlburian Charles Sorley were also dead; a second wave of war poets, who were not public school educated, were not even officers, was coming to the front line. They had begun to realise what the war really entailed. There is certainly no enthusiasm in Isaac Rosenberg's accounts of his decision to join up. His working-class family were fiercely pacifist ('Tolstoylians') and he dared not even admit to them what he had done. He had written to one of his few mentors only days before making the decision: "more men means more war – besides the immorality of joining with no patriotic convictions". But by the time he was in France he could at least tell Laurence Binyon (who would eventually write the introduction to his posthumous volume) that he was determined not to "leave a corner of my consciousness covered up, but saturate myself with the strange and extraordinary new conditions of this life, and it will all refine itself into poetry later on". There was to be no later on, and the few remarkable poems of Rosenberg's that have come down to us are perhaps only the beginning of what he would have achieved. He left no flawless masterpiece, although 'Break of Day in the Trenches' must count as one of the finest poems of the war, a prize that many would give to the longer, more uneven yet more ambitious 'Dead Man's Dump'.

Born on 25th November, 1890, three months after Ivor Gurney (and not so very far away from Gurney's 'patch', in Bristol), Isaac Rosenberg was destined for a short life and a poor one. His father was a hawker, a pedlar, although a very scholarly man, too, keen to impress on his son the richness of his Jewish tradition, which would emerge so strongly in the poet's work, and which was to include just such a sense of 'destiny'. His biographer Jean Liddiard captures something of the boy's complexity when she writes of him:

> ... an immigrant in an alien land, born an orthodox Jew in a Christian culture, a working-class boy with ambitions usually accessible only to the classically educated leisured classes, he was a Jew who abandoned strict orthodoxy, a painter who grew out of sympathy with the major developments of his time, yet who remained a close friend of artists in the forefront of new movements.

Like Ivor Gurney, who also enlisted in 1915, Isaac Rosenberg was to become a master of two arts: in Gurney's case, it was music that singled him out from an early age and gave him a way out of his fairly restricted circumstances; for Rosenberg, it was drawing.

Drawing materials were expensive, but the young Rosenberg was encouraged by teachers and sent to local art classes, even though a boy of his background would be unlikely to have much hope of following a career in the fine arts at this time. In 1905, when the extensive family had eventually relocated to a crowded house in the East End of London, he was apprenticed to an engraver and began to attend evening classes at Birkbeck College, making considerable progress, winning prizes and finding new friends. He came to poetry through gatherings at a local library and through contact with several older women. There is little suggestion of any love affair in Rosenberg's life, but he corresponded candidly with his teachers Alice Wright (from Birkbeck) and particularly Miss Winifrida Seaton (to whom he was introduced at a friend's studio when he was young). To the latter he wrote some time before 1912: "Nobody ever told me what to read or ever put poetry in my way. I don't think I knew what real poetry was till I read Keats a couple of years ago". It was Donne and Emerson, rather than the more fashionable Whitman, whose work particularly struck him. Although painting and drawing were more sociable pursuits, he felt attracted to poetry, inspired by the example of painter-poet Blake: "poetry is his obsession" one of his friends remarked in 1911, "it is only in poetry that he feels himself somebody".

To feel yourself somebody as a writer is quite different from feeling somebody in society and Isaac Rosenberg was always desperately uncomfortable in company ("I'm a very bad talker ... I leave the impression of being a rambling idiot") and his bluntness in dealing with those who tried to help him frequently led him into difficulties. When he was 'taken up' by the wealthy Mrs Herbert Cohen, who helped pay for a term's studies at the Slade School of Fine Art, the result was a falling out because he would not compromise his artistic standards to please her desire for "a more healthy style of work". Similarly, when Rupert Brooke died, he blundered thoughtlessly into Edward Marsh's private grief, nagging him to do more to help him sell paintings. Rosenberg had little taste for fashionable Brooke's "begloried sonnets" which reminded him "too much of flag days", but despite this, Marsh (the editor of the *Georgian Poetry* series of books and an important public figure) became a loyal supporter of the young Stepney poet, even if he did not quite fit the Georgian mould. In Marsh's opinion, Rosenberg was too cavalier about questions of form – and not only poetic form, although that was troubling enough to such a traditionalist. His lack of social graces, coupled with his very un-Brooke-like appearance, made it doubly hard for Rosenberg to establish himself. Yet through the Slade and the offices of one or two enthusiasts, he found himself on the fringes of the literary scene and those who troubled to spend time with him came to appreciate his qualities. In November 1913 Rosenberg was taken to the Café Royal by Mark Gertler, where he met T.E. Hulme and (for the first time) Edward Marsh, whose breakfasts were considered literary hot spots at the time. Ezra Pound became aware of him and made sure that Harriet Monroe took some of these 'Stepney' poems for the influential Chicago magazine, *Poetry.*

Publication on any grander scale was out of the question, but Rosenberg arranged for pamphlets of his work to be printed privately at regular intervals: *Night and Day* (1912), *Youth* (1915) and *Moses* (1916). These, together with one extract from his play *Moses* in

Marsh's third anthology, the American acceptance and one other in a periodical, were the only works of Rosenberg's to be published in his lifetime. It is good to note that as I write this, although the invaluable *Collected Works* is out of print, two new selected editions of his poems and letters have just appeared and a *Complete Poems and Plays* is imminent. Rosenberg the painter was a little more successful, with (for example) five works on display at the Whitechapel Gallery in 1914: his surviving paintings (reproduced in that out-of-print volume) show what a fine portrait artist he was becoming.

In the months leading up to the war, Isaac Rosenberg's health became a problem and he secured assistance from the Jewish Educational Aid Society to spend some time on the south coast, but when he returned to Stepney, things were no better. Consequently, it was decided that he should visit his sister Minnie in South Africa. The JEAS paid his fare and he sailed in June 1914, full of hopes that he would be able to earn a living as a painter in such an exotic location. Sadly, he found Cape Town, though superficially "gorgeous", a very philistine place. It did not move him to write much poetry, although it stirred him to prepare a series of lectures on art in order to inspire the locals.

It was while he was in South Africa that war was declared. When Rosenberg heard the news that "Europe will have just stepped into its bath of blood" he felt no urge at all to take part, but rather suggested sardonically that he would "be waiting with beautiful drying towels of painted canvas". And he wrote a poem, whose final stanza Jon Stallworthy has singled out to demonstrate how much would change in the months to come: "O! ancient crimson curse!/Corrode, consume./ Give back this universe/Its pristine bloom." Like Laurence Binyon and others, Rosenberg sees the war as a winnowing, a purging. It was not so easy to write in those terms from a waterlogged dugout, knee-deep in the stinking remains of "gallant warriors".

The style of Rosenberg's poetry up to this point has been rich and allusive, not to say obscure. Those few contemporaries who bothered to comment on his verse – Gordon Bottomley, Lascelles Abercrombie, big names in their day – tended to mingle praise with much harsh criticism. Rosenberg, of course, welcomed any commentary at all, but was touched and disbelieving when established figures offered genuine appreciation. Marsh, to whom Rosenberg sent most of his work during the war, became increasingly impatient with some of Rosenberg's density and did not really use his influence to promote the young poet to his front rank of Georgians. Later, critics such as Geoffrey Grigson have been even more severe: "I can see next to no merit in the poems," he writes. "How one would like Rosenberg to have been a good poet, how many people have told us that he was a good poet, when he wasn't". Grigson complains of "aesthetic turbulence in an ordinary mind". One can see what he means, but reading through the earlier work there is an increasing sense of a true poet emerging from the shell. The closer we come to the war, the more convincing he seems: not easy, but original and urgently questing to find the right notes for the music in his head. The poet C.H. Sisson, who was so critical of Owen, wrote of how "Rosenberg was bursting with things to say … the tension of Rosenberg's verse arises directly from his fullness with his subject", emphasising that he was "always thinking" and had "urgent imaginative secrets to convey". D.W. Harding, one of his most authoritative champions, values Rosenberg's determination to use the language to help him find what Wallace Stevens called the "plain sense of things"; while Rosenberg himself spoke of aiming for a poetry "where an interesting complexity of thought is kept in tone and right value to the dominating idea so that it is understandable and still ungraspable".

Returning to Stepney from South Africa six months after the outbreak of war, Rosenberg cannot but have been affected by the mood in the capital. Already it was clear that the war was turning into something unexpected: the armies had dug in and the front lines were established. The cavalry was not going to win this war: it would be machine guns and barbed wire, such things as no one had yet put in a poem. No Man's Land had been discovered. So had trench life. Many of Rosenberg's associates and some of his own family had volunteered to have their first taste of it or were planning to. Jean Liddiard captures the atmosphere that must have met him:

> As he walked through London to look up old friends at the
> Café Royal, the familiar pubs, now shuttered and silent in the
> afternoons, roared into noisy life again behind thick curtains
> for the blackout. To Kitchener's imperious finger on the
> hoardings were added a growing number of appeals to women,

"Women of Britain say, Go", and the famous "Daddy, What did you do in the Great War?" ... The daily papers, besides the ever-increasing casualty lists, showed an insistent strain of racial hatred ... Rosenberg was caught between these opposing pressures: the Tolstoyan attitudes of his family ... and the gathering momentum of the war itself.

To be anti-war was to make oneself vulnerable to more than just white feathers, even though Rosenberg had the best of excuses: he was only five feet tall. He tried to get on with his life, painting, writing, and, despite the bad effect it had on his weak lungs, working as an engraver. But all around him the unfit and the over- (or under-) age were trying desperately to become involved. C.E. Montagu apparently dyed his hair black in order to make himself look young enough for service, prompting the painter Nevinson to quip that he was the only man whose hair had turned black overnight – through courage. Rosenberg was more and more isolated, particularly now Edward Marsh himself had lost his position of influence as Churchill was out of government. After the disaster at Loos, a huge recruiting operation was under way, battering at the consciences of those men left at home. There was a new flexibility about who would be eligible: old or young, short or half-blind. Perhaps what finally persuaded Rosenberg was the hope that he would be able to give his mother some money once he signed up, although even that was not as easy as he had hoped.

In October 1915, he disappeared without telling anyone where he had gone and then wrote to the ever-helpful Jewish philanthropist Sydney Schiff, explaining that he had joined the so-called Bantam Battalion – for what we would call today the 'vertically challenged'. It was not to be a happy experience, because he knew he was betraying his family's ideals, but also because the battalion consisted of some of the roughest recruits ("Falstaff's scarecrows were nothing to these," he wrote) and Rosenberg found himself ill-equipped, ill-fed and ill-treated. He was bullied unmercifully and had continual problems with bad feet. In March 1916 he told Abercrombie, "the army is the most detestable invention on earth". Nevertheless, the experience helped him to hone his poetic style even further, to focus on the "definite thought and clear expression" he told Marsh he aspired to. The poem 'August 1914' with its striking "iron, honey, gold" conceit is probably from this period, as is the very naturalistic ten-line sketch, 'The Troop Ship', written after he had endured intensive training and (as part of the 11th Battalion, King's Own Royal Lancasters Regiment) embarked for France. He arrived at the Somme only three weeks after the 1st July offensive.

Life in the trenches was perhaps not as great a shock for Rosenberg as for those who had never known deprivation, but since he was not an officer he found it difficult to find time, space, privacy, warmth or indeed light in which to write poetry. He had to scrounge candle-ends, scraps of paper, pencil-stubs, and did manage to post some work to England for his sister Annie to type out, although he was often "forbidden to send poems home to spare the censor". Given these conditions, the lice, the rats, the stench of death, the continuous noise, the sheer exhaustion, not to mention the various raids and bombardments of so-called action, it is all the more remarkable that Isaac Rosenberg managed to produce in June 1916 one of the great trench poems, presumably after he had done his round of stacking sleepers or digging latrines.

'Break of Day in the Trenches' has just the right title: 'Dawn in the Trenches', 'Sunrise in the Trenches', 'Daybreak in the Trenches' – no, 'Break of Day', as in the breaking of a heart or a promise, the snapping of hope. The way the darkness "crumbles" in the first line suggests the fragmentation of civilisation that will become T.S. Eliot's theme after the war. But we are in a surprisingly theatrical scene, cinematic even, evocative of Stonehenge as much as the trenches. Druids sacrificed humans, and here is the latest such spectacle, updated, the only live audience a rat.

Jon Silkin (in *Out of Battle*) has explored the way in which Rosenberg associates the rat with a malign God. "Sardonic" and "droll" are certainly surprising adjectives, effective because they are so coolly anti-romantic in this most romantic setting of a sunrise and because they suggest a shrugging acceptance of fate. In most of the war poets we are considering, a sense of humour survives in song or anecdote; perhaps it is Rosenberg's essentially unclubbable nature that makes his poetry as grim-lipped as one of his own self-portraits. Here, only the rats can smile at the antics of humans and the humans themselves serve at the rat's "pleasure".

The alliteration and assonance of 'Break of Day in the Trenches' are employed with heavy exaggeration. So, picking a poppy, which should be an act lightly undertaken, is made to pop and sputter like a machine gun. And "the sleeping green between", conjuring the heart of a village or a cricket square or maybe one of Blake's *Songs of Innocence*, sounds absurdly ridiculous since this is the death zone, No Man's Land. "Green" is deformed in the next line to "grin"; the same rat (or rat-god) mocking all that the English public school has raised: "Strong eyes, fine limbs, haughty athletes,/Less chanced than you for life,/Bonds to the whims of murder,/Sprawled in the bowels of the earth,/The torn fields of France." The imagery here makes a latrine of the heroic battlefield, but "torn fields" also suggests the spoiled paper of treaties and signatures. Paper was too scarce in the trenches for Rosenberg to tear up any of his own. But the verb speaks of the destruction of old poetic values: Milton is echoed in "Hurled through still heavens" and Keats' Grecian Urn in the next line, "What quaver—what heart aghast?" The only poetic response is:

> Poppies whose roots are in man's veins
> Drop, and are ever dropping;
> But mine in my ear is safe—
> Just a little white with the dust.

The poppy is in his ear, as is the new poetry – this very poem, with its free verse and startling images. The "break of day" is a new dawn in that sense. It is also the dawn of so much that T.S. Eliot would exploit. If only Isaac Rosenberg had lived to see what Eliot would do with rats, what a retort he might have made to Gerontion, to Burbank and Bleistein. As it was, when 'Break of Day in the Trenches' appeared in the influential magazine *Poetry* in December 1916, two months after its submission, its creator had only just over a year to live.

'Dead Man's Dump' is usually considered to be the other great Rosenberg war poem, although it seems far less fully achieved and it precipitated yet another disagreement with Marsh. It exists in three somewhat different typescripts, the last of which is signed and dated 14th May 1917. What catches our attention is the shocking directness of the middle section, ("a man's brains splattered on/A stretcher-bearer's face") as horrific in its way as Owen's description of a gas attack; and the obsessiveness of the wheel imagery, from the opening, where: "The wheels lurched over sprawled dead/But pained them not, though their bones crunched", to the final 18 lines which feature the word "wheels" six times. What comes to mind is one of the official photographs of the Menin Road, upturned gun carriages rising from the mud and carnage, one wheel among others silhouetted against the smoking sky. We may think of Ixion's perpetually revolving wheel of torment or "wheels within wheels" in the political circles of those who planned the war, the mechanised horror of it all. Or we may think that it was just like a game of roulette. Rosenberg's feeling for destiny was strong and the wheel of fortune is active in this poem, from the moment we realise that it is merely a question of fate who lives and who dies: "Our lucky limbs as on ichor fed,/Immortal seeming ever?"

Rosenberg survived the fearsome winter of 1916-17, cheered by gifts from well-wishers at home, writing wonderful letters and other poems by which he is known. 'A worm fed on the heart of Corinth' shows him a master of the short, dark, Blakean lyric and reminds us (as do the final poems he wrote, of Solomon and Babylon and Lebanon) that he always saw the wider context. He had travelled as well as read books. He had suffered long before he even dreamt of the Great War. Yet he could describe what was just under his nose – 'Louse Hunting' is Rosenberg in most sardonic mood, a very Goya-esque cartoon of men as "gibbering shadows", their "merry limbs in hot Highland fling" – or what was just above his head, as in 'Returning, We Hear the Larks'. The latter poem is one of his best, although after the incomparable: "Death could drop from the dark/ As easily as song –/But song only dropped" the concluding lines' symbolism seems rather mealy-mouthed and Victorian.

Rosenberg was increasingly affected by the cold and wet and forever in trouble with his superiors for breaches of duty such as forgetting his gas mask (punishment: seven days' pack drill) but there were brighter moments, not least of which was his last home leave in September 1917 after 14 months at the front, and one or two spells in hospital during which he could read and write. In November he received the Georgian anthology with an extract from his verse drama *Moses* in it. The story of his last months involves much shifting about: three days in the line, three in support, and much mud and foul weather as 1918 advanced. By March there were rumours of an attack around Ypres and a feeling of inevitabity creeps into his writing. On 11th March he is training near Arras and he is trying to negotiate a transfer to a Jewish regiment. On 19th he is sent to the Greenland Hill sector, Arras and on 23rd his battalion bears the brunt of a German assault. A full-scale attack on 28th brings enormous losses. Three days later, on the last day of March, Isaac Rosenberg was sent out on a night patrol and was killed some time before break of day on 1st April 1918. He was buried on the battlefield, probably at Northumberland Cemetery, Fampoux, and subsequently removed along with nine other bodies to Bailleul Road East Cemetery, where a headstone ("Buried near this spot") gives his name, with "Artist and Poet" added at the request of his family.

An edition of Rosenberg's poems, edited by Gordon Bottomley, appeared in 1922 and Laurence Binyon's memoir in that volume recalls his first encounter with the poet 10 years earlier:

> … a boy with an unusual mixture of self-reliance and modesty. Indeed, no one could have had a more independent nature. Obviously sensitive, he was not touchy or aggressive. Possessed of vivid enthusiasms, he was shy in speech. One found in talk how strangely little of second-hand (in one of his age) there was to his opinions, how fresh a mind he brought to what he saw and read. There was an odd kind of charm in his manner which came from his earnest transparent sincerity.

Binyon would have been surprised to know how far that shy boy's reputation has advanced beyond his own in the last 80 years, and how much greater a loss Rosenberg's death was than many realised at the time. He may have left only one or two fully mature poems, but he showed greater potential than any. The Australian, Les Murray, writes along similar lines in his level-headed review of the *Collected Works* and even suggests that Rosenberg "might have allowed English poetry to renew itself in a native way through his development (…) without the alien and wrenching effects of Eliot's and Pound's Franco-American modernism". This is something that later poets soon came to recognise, particularly the greatest poet of the next war, Keith

Douglas, whose 'Desert Flowers' begins: "Living in a wide landscape are the flowers –/Rosenberg I only repeat what you were saying".

Further Reading

Rosenberg:

The Complete Poems and Plays of Isaac Rosenberg (ed. Vivian Noakes, OUP, 2004)

The Collected Works of Isaac Rosenberg (ed. Ian Parsons, Chatto & Windus, 1984)

Selected Poems and Letters (ed. Jean Liddiard, Enitharmon, 2003)

* * *

Grigson, Geoffrey, *Blessings, Kicks and Curses* (Allison and Busby, 1982)

Harding, D.W., *Experience Into Words* (Chatto & Windus, 1963)

Liddiard, Jean, *Isaac Rosenberg: the Half-Used Life* (Gollancz, 1975)

Murray, Les, *The Paperbark Tree* (Minerva, 1993)

Silkin, Jon, *Out of Battle* (Routledge and Kegan Paul, 1972)

Sisson, C.H., *English Poetry 1900-1950* (Carcanet, 1981)

3

Edward Thomas 1878-1917

What everyone remembers about Edward Thomas is that he did not write any poetry for most of his life, then just as the war broke out he was persuaded by Robert Frost to try. In the two years before his death on Vimy Ridge, he produced the 144 poems by which he is known today: a Brueghel canvas where quirky, unexpected detail and human interest are set against a meticulously observed pastoral landscape. To read all the poems straight through is to find oneself in another country, neither England nor France, but a dreamland full of uncertainty and deceptiveness. Thomas himself described the writing process as "a dull blindfold journey through a strange lovely land: I seem to take what I write from the dictation of someone else". The native language of this land is always pushing further and further into syntactical ambiguity: "raids on the inarticulate" in more ways than T.S. Eliot could have imagined, even in his own 'Waste Land'. There is something of *Through the Looking Glass* about so many bizarrely conducted conversations ('As the Team's Head-Brass', 'The Other') and the many unanswerable riddles Thomas' world presents. Nothing is what it seems, but dissolves even as we look at it. Like the poet in 'The Glory', we "cannot bite the day to the core". Here, the apparent gleam of a flower could prove to be mere bird-dung or "fresh-cut faggot ends". The overlooked and the undervalued suddenly grow out of all proportion – an abandoned barn, an old rain butt with its nettles, a deserted railway station, a combe. a copse, a chalk pit. 'Thomasland' is recognisable, too, by what is not there: Bob's Lane, but where is Bob? Birdsong, but the bird is unknown. And who is this mysterious "Other", this indefinable archetype, Lob?

Such characters disappear into the names of Thomas' mental landscapes:

> The man you saw, – Lob-lie-by-the-fire, Jack Cade,
> Jack Smith, Jack Moon, poor Jack of every trade,
> Young Jack, or old Jack, or Jack What-d'ye-call,
> Jack-in-the-hedge, or Robin-run-by-the-wall,
> Robin Hood, Ragged Robin, lazy Bob,
> One of the lords of No Man's Land, good Lob –
>
> 'Lob'

As Thomas himself hears more and more of the real No Man's Land in Europe, the landscapes he creates become increasingly depopulated: cherry trees bend over "strewing the grass as for a wedding/This early May morn when there is none to wed" just as in 'In Memoriam [Easter 1915]':

> The flowers left thick at nightfall in the wood
> This Eastertide call into mind the men,
> Now far from home, who, with their sweethearts, should
> Have gathered them and will do never again.

Unlike many of the poets considered here, Edward Thomas does not use his poetry to describe trench life, even though he experienced it and his terse, vivid War Diary shows us what he had to endure and also how effortlessly he moved from the language of natural history to that of warfare, even describing the shells as starlings and the "flap"(like a bird's wing) of their explosion:

> 20th [March 1917]: Stiff deep mud all the way up and shelled as we started. Telegraph Hill as quiet as if only rabbits lived there. I took revolver and left this diary behind in case. For it is very exposed and only a few Cornwalls and MGC [Machine Gun Corps] about. But Hun shelled chiefly over our heads into Beaurains all night – like starlings returning 20 or 30 a minute. Horrible flap of 5.9 a little along the trench. Rain and mud and I've to stay till I am relieved tomorrow … A terribly long night and cold.

25

But all Thomas' poems were written before he went to France, and he only knew of the trenches what he had read and heard. His fears and imaginings about the Western Front must have contributed to the way he painted the English landscape. Even the scene he evokes in his very first poem, 'Up in the Wind', anticipates the lines of trenches and No Man's Land: a single line of road running for "eleven houseless miles", once "the border of waste".

There is no doubt that the war simplified and focused a life that was increasingly complex, mired in melancholia and Yeatsian 'responsibilities'. Yet in many ways Edward Thomas should have been content. By the time he enlisted he was a widely respected critic and travel writer, who had a rich variety of literary friendships as well as a stable and loving family life. He had met Helen Noble when he was still a teenager, unsociable, fond of solitary walking and swimming, ill at ease in the London suburbs, haunted by the beauty of Wales, possessed by a passion for natural history, "something in him ever inexpressible" as one of his associates from that time put it. The greatest influence on him was one 'Dad Uzzell' (how different from his real 'Dad') a Lob-figure who fired his love of the countryside. But Edward immediately warmed to Helen, who was the daughter of a usefully influential journalist. Her loyalty to Edward, to his genius and to their shared belief in freedom and honesty would prove extraordinarily impressive. Her memoirs *As It Was* and *World Without End* are an enduring tribute to the relationship, and how it survived Edward's depressions, nocturnal wanderings and occasional roving eye. Her tolerance when he becomes infatuated with a 17-year-old ("Well never mind sweetheart, perhaps she loves you") is surely beyond the call of duty. He knew what she was putting up with: "My wife could be the happiest women on earth," he wrote, "and I won't let her".

Edward studied at Lincoln College, Oxford, where he learnt to "topple into bed on the verge of drunkenness ... swear: use slang creditably: howl choruses ... be heartily sick", to acquire a reputation for being foul-mouthed and difficult, and even to contract a gonococcal infection as a result of one of his many drinking binges. He also managed to get Helen pregnant. They married secretly on 20th June 1899 and spent many years shifting from rented house to house, struggling with poverty, with Edward frequently separated from

Helen. Further pregnancies made things worse, as Thomas wrote in one of his many letters to his wife: "It would be insanity to go about arcadizing with bankruptcy and the gutter ahead". Yet although he felt unable to write potboilers and only once attempted a novel (*The Happy-Go-Lucky Morgans*) he was making contacts in literary circles in London and establishing a name for himself as a nature writer. Since this paid very badly, he was also trying to make a living by book reviewing, with the occasional foray into Civil Service work. Two thirds of the reviews he wrote are carefully preserved in family scrap-books: at least 1200 of them. In one two-month period alone he wrote more than 40, all the while working to meet the deadline on his current prose book. Although Ezra Pound thought that Thomas the critic had "no vinegar in his veins", his poetry reviews are some of the sharpest ever written and seldom betray the kind of pressure they were written under. In fact, if Thomas had anything in his veins it was probably laudanum, which he took increasingly when he had deadlines to meet. He felt continual frustration at the "little leisure (from reviewing and much thinking about money) left me to write my best in", but it did not damage his judgement. He recognised immediately, for example, that Frost's *North of Boston* was "one of the most revolutionary books of modern times, but one of the quietest and least aggressive" and he saw that the poet Pound himself would "reach we know not where ... somewhere far away in the unexplored".

Thomas' nature writing formed (as his biographer R. George Thomas puts it) "the direct channel through which flowed that undercurrent of prose-poems which eventually emerged as his poetry". The "prose-poem" as such might indeed have appealed to him had it not been a virtually non-existent form at that time. In a review of Baudelaire in 1906, Thomas writes of it as something "rarely attempted ... No writer of repute has anything to do with it". So he treated this hack work as a craftsman might "the dull routine of country employment ..." enjoying (R. George Thomas suggests) "the craftsman's welcome relief from paid labour at a day's end". It was *In Pursuit of Spring,* with its mysterious 'Other Man' and its pagan anti-Christian leanings, its account of a pursuit of the self as much as Spring, that Robert Frost thought so close to the speech rhythms of good poetry. Thomas thought so himself now and then but more often was scathing about his 'travel' books on Oxford and

Wales and *The Heart of England* (which he called "Borrow and Jefferies sans testicles and guts") written "against time and by order". He longed to "let the wind and sun do my thinking for me". But it was not only time he battled with: there were the distractions of noisy young children and family responsibilities, not to mention his increasing unease with Helen, compensated for by a deepening friendship with Eleanor Farjeon, who would type out many of his poems for him. There was also his own melancholia, his suicidal tendencies, which led to consultations with a Jungian analyst, Godwin Baynes, in 1912. Interestingly, even two years before the outbreak of war, Thomas is writing how he has "that feeling of one waiting to begin a race – waiting with all one's ears and nerves and muscles for the word 'go' ..."

The Thomases eventually settled at Steep, Hampshire, which was near enough to Bedales School for the children. It was here, on a windy site above the Shoulder of Mutton, that many of the early poems were drafted, in response to Frost's insistence that he drag himself "out from under the heap of his own work in prose" and try "verse form in exactly the same cadence" as some of the paragraphs from *In Pursuit of Spring*. It may well be, as R. George Thomas believes, that Thomas would have turned to verse even without this prompting. Frost's intervention was like the gunshot in Sarajevo: the Great War would begin one way or another, and so would Edward Thomas' great poetry. Or Edward Eastaway's – since that is the Welsh family name he asked Gordon Bottomley to publish his poetry under. Nevertheless, the friendship between Frost and Thomas was genuine and heartfelt. Thomas was, of course, the establishment figure, Frost an unknown American, when they met in October 1913. By February 1914, they were soulmates and in April a week-long visit by Thomas to Frost's Gloucestershire cottage, Little Iddens, only reinforced their shared views on language and poetry. When Thomas died, Frost wrote to Amy Lowell: " ... the closest I ever came to anyone in England or anywhere else in the world I think was with Edward Thomas, who was killed at Vimy last Spring. He more than anyone else was accessory to what I had done and was doing".

Once war was declared, there was less demand for the kind of journalism Edward Thomas wrote. He did produce some appropriately 'patriotic' anthologies, a few articles of wartime interest for

English Review and he persevered with his biography of Marlborough, but "something, I felt, had to be done before I could look again composedly at English landscape". He was tormented with guilt and knew that he would have to enlist – although Frost was trying to lure him to America instead. By November 1914, he had begun writing poems and (while recovering from an injured ankle) completed 16 by the New Year, then another 60 before the end of May. Another group of 10 was written in June and July as he made the final decision: "Last week I had screwed myself up to the point of believing I should come out to America ... But I have altered my mind. I am going to enlist on Wednesday". Thus, he joined the Artists' Rifles and began a new life. He knew precisely why he was doing so and demonstrated the belief to Eleanor Farjeon when she asked what he was fighting for by stooping to pick up (as she describes it) "a pinch of earth: 'Literally, for this.' He crumbled it between finger and thumb and let it fall". There would be less time for poetry; but he had already composed over half of his *Collected Poems*. Frost was disappointed that he could not come to America, but recognised that the war was making "some sort of new man and poet out of Edward Thomas".

Edward Thomas may well have been making a map-reader out of Wilfred Owen, since he was soon promoted to Lance Corporal and set to instructing young officers in map skills at Hare Hall Camp, Romford, at the very time Owen was there (November 1915). Thomas could have stayed in England doing this. He was indeed as happy at Hare Hall as Edward Thomas ever could be and composed over 40 poems there, few of which betray any sense of what he was doing at the time. The fatigue and routine of the camp somehow released in him the resources that fed his poetry ("I can sometimes get the hut empty and write"). He was clearly a very fine soldier and communicator: there are innumerable testimonials to his efficiency, although he was perhaps a little reluctant to impose discipline. But with characteristic restlessness, keen to see what was going on 'out there', determined (as he wrote to Frost) to "do something if I am discovered to be of any use, but in any case to be made to run risks, to be put through it", he decided to train as an officer cadet with the Royal Artillery. He left Hare Hall in August and found himself in Trowbridge, reassuringly near to the land of his heart, and to his family.

Here he wrote some of his last poems, including 'Lights Out'. This poem is characteristic of a certain portion of Edward Thomas' war poetry in that it does not appear to be about the war at all: yet the title is a military bugle-call and dusk was as crucial a time as dawn for soldiers (see Paul Fussell's *The Great War and Modern Memory*). Once we know what the poet was on the verge of entering, how much he had heard from returning soldiers about the disaster of the Somme, we read 'Lights Out' rather differently. The way the syntax plays against the line-breaks in the opening stanza while the rhyme-words lap and lick at the edge is typical. Thomas wondered whether he had over-emphasised the forest metaphor (it is a heavy trochaic stress), but claimed that the poem "sums up what I have often thought at that call". Very different responses to such calls turn up in the poem beginning "No one cares less than I ..." and in 'The Trumpet'.

A few of Thomas' poems just mention the war in passing (see 'Blenheim Oranges') or bring it in at the end: so 'Roads', after exploring how much he loves them, concludes "Now all roads lead to France"; or in 'The Owl', with its superbly sinuous uncoiling sentence and its ominous mood, the call of the owl, traditionally a portent of death, is "Shaken out long and clear upon the hill" as if it were salt. Salt is essential to life, but it preserves dead carcasses, too. So the poem finishes: "And salted was my food, and my repose,/ Salted and sobered, too, by the bird's voice/Speaking for all who lay under the stars,/Soldiers and poor, unable to rejoice." This is Thomas' 'Ode to a Nightingale': as the darkness invited Keats, so Thomas the nightwalker is invigorated by the night-call of death, imagining a dark emissary from the trenches. In 'Rain' the gloomy weather sets the poet wondering once again about those who might be lying helplessly in No Man's Land (though he doesn't use the term). It is interesting how a complex and ambiguous attitude to rain muddies the final pages of *In Pursuit of Spring,* where Thomas wonders only half in fun why such a bedraggled nation has "never produced anything to keep us dry and comfortable in rain ... Real outdoor people" he says, " ... have done nothing to solve our difficulties. They have not written poetry for us, they have not made waterproofs for us. They do not read our poetry, they do not wear our waterproofs ..." In this poem, he captures the dreary monotony of warfare (and after all 90 per cent of the experience was boredom for most men), dragging Laurence Binyon's favourite heroic word "myriad" down into the mud where the dead lie "Like a cold water among broken reeds,/Myriads of broken reeds all still and stiff" and concluding with the anything but rousing verb "disappoint".

Other Thomas poems take the distant view of war, as when he unearths an old soldier's clay pipe in 'Digging[2]' and in 'February Afternoon [Sonnet 2]', where "men strike and bear the stroke/Of war as ever, audacious or resigned,/And God still sits aloft in the array/That we have wrought him, stone-deaf and stone-blind." Then there is the close-up, the snapshot: the passing soldiers, like little characters in the corner of the Brueghel: "This ploughman dead in battle ..." ('A Private'), is Thomas' Drummer Hodge. He keeps the secret of his favourite Wiltshire hawthorn bush as well as "where now at last he sleeps/More sound in France". In 'Tears', Thomas describes a send-off of many young Hodges and Shropshire lads, "young English countrymen,/Fair-haired and ruddy, in white tunics" who "told me truths I had not dreamed". Only in one not altogether successful poem does Thomas confront the war emotionally and head-on: 'This is No Case of Petty Right or Wrong' was sparked by an argument with his father and it shows Thomas in passionate mood, willing to cheer for his country but not to hate the Kaiser just for the sake of it.

While several poems merely emphasise the increasing emptiness of the landscape as men go off to war – as in 'Fifty Faggots', where the poet's eye lights on a wood-pile with no one to burn them (very similar, this, to Frost's 'The Wood-Pile') – perhaps Thomas' best war poems are the conversations, the encounters with humanity: 'It was Upon a July Evening', 'Home', 'Man and Dog' anticipate the greatest of them, 'As the Team's Head-Brass'. In this wonderful loose blank verse poem, the steady rhythm of the ploughing captured by the back-forth iambic line, the good-humoured note of the continually interrupted conversation, and the immoveable presence of the English Elm, crown resting on the earth, suggest Thomas Hardy's lines: "Only a man harrowing clods/In slow silent walk ... Yet this will go onward the same/Though Dynasties pass." The rhythms of the country seem unstoppable: the lovers disappear into the wood to a precise iambic rhythm, come out again somewhat stirred, metrically speaking. The peasant has time for the poet ("Instead of treading me down"), but has to keep on working. Of course, they talk about the war. The elm is still there because there is no one to take it away: "a good few" have been lost from this community:

Only two teams work on the farm this year.
One of my mates is dead. The second day
In France they killed him. It was back in March,
The very night of the blizzard, too. Now if
He had stayed here we should have moved the tree.

So the moving of the fallen elm comes to represent some revolutionary aspiration, some need for change which has been set aside by the war. Perhaps that fallen crown of the elm is what we are supposed to dwell on, or the flashing of all that "brass". The political enthusiasms of Edward Thomas' father are somewhere buried in this poem. And maybe an anger the equal of Siegfried Sassoon's. But reading it today, what we feel is the capturing of a moment of transformation (as the field is being transformed by the plough). A new England will indeed rise up, as Thomas sardonically suggested in 'This is No Case ...' We know now just how cataclysmic the First World War proved for English society. Neither poet nor ploughman could possibly be aware of this, but the future has been broadcast by the end of these 36 lines.

Edward Thomas commemorated his friendship with Frost in 'The Sun Used to Shine' (as Frost remembered him in 'To E.T.'), a poem which is one of Thomas' best self-portraits and which invites us to see the war as a vicious wasp, eating at "the yellow flavorous coat" of a peacetime apple but at the same time something utterly unreal and removed, as madly transient as moonlight on the water, as inevitably gone "to the cider-heap as of no worth" as those fallen apples in Frost's 'After Apple-Picking'. The whole poem drifts into a Samuel Palmer orchard scene or a Vaughan Williams epilogue:

... Nevertheless, our eyes

Could as well imagine the Crusades
Or Caesar's battles. Everything
To faintness like those rumours fades—
Like the brook's water glittering

Under the moonlight—like those walks
Now—like us two that took them, and
The fallen apples, all the talks
And silences—like memory's sand

When the tide covers it late or soon,
And other men through other flowers
In those fields under the same moon
Go talking and have easy hours.

The epilogue to Edward Thomas' own life involves preparations
at Wanstrow, Somerset, Salisbury Plain and Lydd together with a
few lighter moments: final visits to parents, a ramble with Helen,
calling on his his daughter Myfanwy, a sing-song at the poet Gordon
Bottomley's ("he always sang when he came to us"), sketching his
penultimate poem 'Out in the Dark', learning to ride a motorbike,
practising compass-setting and range-finding for the guns, beginning
his War Diary. In the diary he is as quick to note the men's use of the
'f'-word and the lively graffiti on the urinals as he is to wax lyrical
about his final bike ride across the downs before embarkation. The
exhilaration of this last jaunt through an English landscape is palpable
as he notes the "hedgeless roads over long sloping downs with woods
and sprinkled thorns, carved with old tracks which junipers line – an
owl and many rabbits – a clear pale sky and but a faint sunset – a
long twilight lasting till 6".

He had felt certain he would be sent to the Somme, but found
himself at the end of January 1917 on the Arras Road, establishing
observation posts. All this is most vividly captured in his letters to
Frost:

> We had some shells very near us, but were not sniped at. I
> could see the German lines very clear but not a movement
> anywhere, nothing but posts sticking out of the snow with
> barbed wire, bare trees broken and dead and half ruined
> houses. The only living men we met at bends in trenches,
> eating or carrying food or smoking. One dead man lay under
> a railway arch so stiff and neat (with a covering of sacking)
> that I only slowly remembered he was dead.

Elsewhere he tells Frost: "I should like to be a poet, just as I
should like to live, but I know as much about my chances in either
case". There is a sense of foreboding, of inescapable fate in much of
what happens in Edward Thomas' last weeks. He had worked at HQ
and seen the plans for the Easter Offensive. He knew that April would
be the cruellest month, long before T.S. Eliot wrote the words.

The run-up to the attack was busy, but he kept reading Shakespeare (the *Sonnets* and *Tragedies*) and writing letters, wondering (to his son Merfyn) why "some men get hit and some don't", or describing nights in the mud and cold and the futile missions he had to undertake, such as trying to climb a chimney in order to see if it would be a useful observation point. He failed this particular challenge, yet for all the unease and fatalism in his last letters, he feels "surer of some primitive things that one has to get sure of, about oneself and other people" adding "I doubt if anybody here thinks less of home than I do and yet I doubt if anybody loves it more".

Edward Thomas was killed by a stray shell – probably what we would call today 'friendly fire' – at the Beaurains Observation Post, at 7.36 a.m. on 9th April. As his daughter Myfanwy describes it: "His body was quite untouched and the war diary in his pocket bore strange sea-shell-like markings as though it had undergone tremendous and violent pressure". Helen's last letter to him was also found on his body. She in turn received a moving account from his CO, Major Lushington, in which he described how "the sun came out and the guns round seemed to stop firing for a short time" as they laid the poet to rest. Lushington also told her how Edward had always gone about his work "quietly and ordinarily as if nothing was happening. I wish I could convey to you the picture of him, a picture we had all learnt to love, of the old clay pipe, gum boots, oilskin coat and steel helmet ..." It is oddly reminiscent of the doomed character of loyal Osborne in R.C. Sherriff's keynote play of the war, *Journey's End*, older than most around him, loved and respected, an old stager, sitting reading Lewis Carroll's *Alice* as the senseless attack approached: "How cheerfully he seems to grin,/How neatly spreads his claws,/And welcomes little fishes in/With gently smiling jaws!" His comrade, the simple-minded Trotter, says he sees no point in the lines; to which Osborne replies: "Exactly. That's just the point."

Further Reading

Thomas:

Collected Poems of Edward Thomas (with *War Diary*) (ed. R. George Thomas, OUP, 1978)

A Language Not to be Betrayed, Selected Prose of Edward Thomas (ed. Edna Longley, Carcanet, 1981)

In Pursuit of Spring (Laurel Books, 2002)

* * *

Farjeon, Eleanor, *Edward Thomas: the Last Four Years* (OUP, 1979)

Motion, Andrew, *The Poetry of Edward Thomas* (London: Routledge and Kegan Paul, 1980)

Smith, Stan, *Edward Thomas* (Faber Critical Guide, 1986)

Thomas, Helen, *As It Was* and *World Without End* (Faber, 1956)

Thomas, R. George, *Edward Thomas* (OUP, 1985)

4

Ivor Gurney 1890-1937

From Arnold Bax to Michael Tippett, there are plenty of examples of composers who have tried to be poets and even some of poets who wished to be composers, but there are very few between the two Elizabethan ages who have showed anything like genius in both spheres. Without wishing to disparage Bob Dylan, Paul McCartney or indeed Thomas Campion, Ivor Gurney is unusual today in that one can go to a bookshop and buy a volume of his poetry or go to a music shop and buy a CD of his songs. Indeed, it was the composer Gerald Finzi who was chiefly responsible for sorting through Gurney's manuscripts and keeping his work in the public domain, a task which proved daunting (see Stephen Banford's biography of Finzi): editors even today are struggling to make sense of all the variant manuscripts, corrections and revisions. Gurney's early songs struck listeners with a Schubertian simplicity. Having heard 'Sleep' performed in York, Finzi wrote of the "incandescence in his songs that tells of something burning too brightly to last, such as you see in the filament of an electric bulb before it burns out". Gurney only ever set one of his own poems to music, the touching two stanzas of 'Song', composed in March 1917 while sheltering in a ruined mausoleum in Caulaincourt:

> Only the wanderer
> Knows England's graces,
> Or can anew see clear
> Familiar faces.

And who loves joy as he
That dwells in shadows?
Do not forget me quite,
O Severn meadows.

Even here (and this poem is an early one, from his first book) we see the preoccupations and paradoxes: he wished to be a Schubertian wanderer, but needed to know that his home meadows would wait for him. It is hardly surprising that the experience of trench life, while superficially invigorating to him, was also troubling at a much deeper level. The soldier cannot wander, unless in his mind; he sees meadows, but they are not his and they are being torn apart. Already the "shadows" had an appeal for Ivor Gurney.

There has been a revolution in Gurney studies in the last 20 years, following the publication of Michael Hurd's brief life, *The Ordeal of Ivor Gurney* and then a definitive *Collected Poems* in which P.J. Kavanagh corrected the misprints (which were "almost everywhere") so removing many of what Finzi called the poet's "queernesses". Since then, George Walter and R.K.R. Thornton have edited a series of individual volumes which show the full bewildering range of Gurney's poetic achievement. *Best Poems and The Book of Five Makings* in particular shows how obsessively Gurney reworked his verse, almost always adding to it, even if that meant wrecking the metre. "Shall you be poetry,/Or tell truth?" he asks in 'First Poem', and he frequently comes down on the side of truth. In 'The Nightingales' he is implicitly scoffing at Keats' conclusions in his 'Ode', when he writes (here quoted with the original insertions and a deletion underlined): "How could I think such beautiful; or gather the lies/utter false the lies//Fit for verse, it was only bird-song". It is not possible in a short study such as this to refer to all such alternative readings, and the new edition of *Collected Poems* (2004) will make the latest thinking more widely available, but the student of Gurney's work should be aware that there is frequently a good deal of editorial input in the texts that they read – but, then, that is also true of Shakespeare.

Ivor Gurney's life began in 1890 in Gloucester, a city which became womb, nursemaid, muse and even regiment to him. His musical abilities were spotted early (a family piano was acquired when he was six; he joined the cathedral choir at ten) and he attended the Royal College of Music, where he was already perceived as an eccentric and was nicknamed Schubert. He was taught by Stanford, who thought him the most promising of all his students (they included Vaughan Williams!) but also the least teachable. Here, Gurney came to know Marion Scott, the musicologist who would be one of his chief supporters, although she also proved a frustrating hoarder of precious manuscripts. In 1912, he began composing songs and poetry came to him the following year "with far less effort than the other".

Had the war not intervened, his life might have been very different, although recently writers have suggested that the seeds of his breakdown were there from the start, "buried deeper and more fundamentally in Gurney's own nature", as Michael Hurd puts it, and George Walter (in his introduction to *Rewards of Wonder*) cites Gordon Claridge's work on the psychopathology of creativity as evidence that the poet suffered from "a long-standing illness of a severely schizophrenic type" rather than the neurasthenia he was diagnosed with at the time.

It took Gurney two attempts to join the army, because of poor eyesight and he filled in the time working as an organist in High Wycombe, where he befriended the Chapman family (particularly the eldest daughter) to whom he would write the lively, witty letters collected in *Stars in a Dark Night*. But on 9th February 1915 he joined his beloved Gloucester Regiment and the following year found himself on the Western Front, suddenly open to (as John Lucas puts it) the "contradictions or confusions out of which much of his best poetry is made". War intensified all experience – even appreciation of music, as in the early lyric 'Bach and the Sentry':

> When I return, and to real music-making,
> And play that Prelude, how will it happen then?
> Shall I feel as I felt, a sentry hardly waking,
> With a dull sense of No Man's Land again?

Many of Gurney's strongest poems are retrospective, and the best are about these early experiences of trench life. 'First March', for example, captures the slogging, numbing monotony of marching (the text quoted is from Kavanagh's *Collected*; George Walter's in *Rewards of Wonder* is much more cluttered in its quest for 'truth'):

> ... it was I
> Who stared for body-ease at the grey sky
> And watched in grind of pain the monotony
> Of grit road metal slide underneath by.
> To get there being the one way not to die.

'First Time In' exists in two 'versions', both included in the *Collected,* and both fine, particularly the shorter one ("After the dread tales ..."): they are two quite different poems about the same obviously significant experience of being welcomed by a group of Welsh soldiers, who "sang us Welsh things, and changed all former notions/To human hopeful things". "Things" is one of Gurney's favourite words: it is the crux of a much anthologised earlier poem, 'To His Love', that marks his shift away from the Georgians, when after fairly conventional elegiacs ("violets of pride"), he suddenly begs that the flowers hide "that red wet/Thing I must somehow forget" and the word also returns three times in 'Sonnet, September, 1922', which Kavanagh calls "extraordinary and unforgettable". The use of "things" in 'First Time In' suggests something tangible to cling to "after the dread tales and red yarns of the Line". Characteristically, the rhymes tend to drive this poem; the undisguised relish for rhyme and extravagant language, including compound nouns ("line-pangs"), was learnt from Hopkins, although later Whitman would be more of an influence.

A reading of Ivor Gurney's war poetry is a guided tour of the towns and villages he was sent to on the Western Front: Riez Bailleul, La Gorgue, Neuve Chappelle, Robecq, Gonnehem; Grandcourt, Aveluy, Ovillers ... For a poet of place, fighting battles that swarmed obsessively around particular places, such names could not but etch themselves on his consciousness. Like John Clare, Gurney's sense of himself came to depend on a fidelity to particular spots: it was the maps of Gloucestershire that Edward Thomas' widow, Helen, brought him to pore over that restored him briefly to sanity towards the end of his life. Correspondingly, to witness a rural landscape torn apart by shelling must have been a torment for a poet whose mind was made up of just such a landscape. To be at the Somme or at Ypres (and Gurney was in both) was to be involved in a ghastly act of violence on the language itself. Yet he had to revisit those places in his poetry – partly, as modern psychiatry would suggest, for therapeutic reasons. "I find ballad making very grateful and comforting to the mind," he writes in a letter to Marion Scott in 1915, "and to praise one's own county makes it not the less joyous".

He found it difficult and perhaps unnecessary to separate Gloucestershire fields from those of France or Flanders; after all, the troops were organised into regiments from the various counties (a practice that proved disastrous for propaganda as swathes of obituaries appeared in local papers) and Gurney wrote about the voices of the soldiers in the battlefield as if they somehow personified their homes: "No more to march happy with such good comrades ... Nor to hear Gloucester with Stroud debating the lack/Of goodliness or virtue in girls on farmlands./Nor to hear Cheltenham hurling at Cotswold demands/Of civilization; nor west Severn joking at east Severn?" ('Farewell'). In 'Behind the Line' he writes: "I suppose France this morning is as white as here/High white clouds veiling the sun ..." and in 'Mist on Meadows': "Mist lies heavy on English meadows/ As ever on Ypres ...": to him, they were both lands of dream, of imagination; he could reach neither. Yet through the mist of distance, far from hills and meadows, far from dug-outs and shell-holes, when he was in an asylum in Dartford, he could write about these places with uncanny vividness. In fact, it is not always easy to tell which war poems of Gurney's are written on the Front: those "recollected in tranquillity" often have a hectic air of reportage about them, and some written amidst the action have a whiff of the midnight oil. Gurney wrote good poems and bad poems all his life, but place was always the most powerful source of inspiration, and – as when he encounters the "rooted" Welshmen in 'First Time In' – of reassurance.

Naturally, it mattered a great deal what kind of place you ended up in as a soldier on the Western Front. A slight shift in one direction or another could mean life or death. That is why Private Gurney, following his instinct, refuses the invitation in 'The Silent One' from an officer with an out-of-place "finicking accent" (contrasting with the friendly, but displaced "Bucks accent" of the wounded man out on the wires): "Do you think you might crawl through there, there's a hole" ... "I'm afraid not, Sir." He knows the importance of judging this correctly, of knowing which place is the safest, which is why so much hinges on the discussion in 'Of Grandcourt':

Rain there was – tired and weak I was, glad for an end.
But one spoke to me – one I liked well as friend,
'Let's volunteer for the Front Line – many others won't.
I'll volunteer, it's better being there than here.'
But I had seen too many ditches and stood too long
Feeling my feet freeze …

The narrator concludes that "Stars looked as well from second as from first line holes".

All the while he was being shifted from place to place, Gurney was composing songs, poems and wonderful letters. He is ahead of his time in so many ways, his judgements on other writers, as John Lucas points out, "astonishingly sure … he came unfailingly to recognise the poets who mattered, who could be of use to him". Take the views he expresses on Rupert Brooke, which are much more common now (see Andrew Motion's introduction to his recent anthology, *First World War Poems*), than when Gurney was writing: "It seems to me that Rupert Brooke would not have improved with age, would not have broadened; his manner had become a mannerism, both in rhythm and diction. I do not like it …"

Of course, Gurney has his mannerisms: missing out conjunctions and prepositions, beginning with an exclamation ("What? to have had gas …"), refusal to smooth out "queerness and untidiness", but instead to elide and compress – but all this is his originality. We hear above all a distinctive new voice, not particularly rich in metaphor (he is no imagist), but relishing rhyme and the ebb and flow of rhythms, bursting the banks of mere metre. His voice sounds from his innermost being and so the poetry is troubled and troubling, as he was himself. As P.J. Kavanagh puts it in his invaluable original introduction to the *Collected Poems*, "his faithfulness to meaning is allowed to yield its own music". The best commentary on Ivor Gurney's style is in his own poetry, where he is much concerned with questions of craftsmanship even in poems such as 'The Lock-Keeper', which are not overtly 'about poetry'. Certainly, Gurney's poems improve as he learns the craft, but some of his earlier pieces from his first published book, *Severn and Somme* (1917), are still powerful, notably the premonitory 'Ballad of the Three Spectres' with its obsessive "ee" rhyme – although it is a pity it has to end on the quaint "spake verity" after the neat dovetailing of Blighty and Picardy.

Ivor Gurney was in at the end of the Battle of the Somme, then after training at Varennes found himself in 1917 at the Arras front in the reserve for 'Third Ypres': a machine-gunner. He spent some time in hospital after receiving a wound in the arm, then was gassed on 10th September near Passchendaele and was considered bad enough to be sent back home. He was put in an Edinburgh hospital (not Craiglockhart) where he immediately fell in love with a VAD nurse, Annie Drummond, who rejected him but whom he clung to in his writings, associating her in characteristically cryptic fashion with the Elizabethan poet Drummond of Hawthornden. Gurney's poetry is full of such private signs and double meanings. There was an air of furtiveness about his being in Blighty at all and he throws in the occasional "wink, wink" or mention of a "wangle" when writing about the gassing. As Michael Hurd writes, "at a time when mustard gas could blister the skin and strip the bronchial tubes of mucous membrane ... Gurney's encounter must surely have been very mild" and it could be (as the Holts suggest) that he "and some friends sheltered in an abandoned dug-out in which there were still traces of gas from a previous attack, hence the mildness of his symptoms".

Despite the moments of exhilaration, despite his love of his comrades, Gurney was anything but a natural soldier and it would be quite in character for him to "wangle" his way back home. Kavanagh even thinks that he barely took the war seriously. The poem 'Bohemians', read as a self-portrait, sums up his attitude, with its wry use of an officer's tone in its opening line: "Certain people would not clean their buttons ..." Michael Hurd quotes various examples of how exasperated his sergeant-major became with him, while emphasising the trouble that was taken to avoid him getting into trouble. Gurney was recognised as being different and in need of protection. Yet the poetry shows that he could tell a hawk from a handsaw. 'Swift and Slow' begins:

> Death swooped suddenly on men in Flanders
> There were no tweedledees or handy-danders
> The skull was cleft, the life went out from it
> And glory in a family tale was set.

Here is Gurney's unique brand of quirky colloquialism and gallows humour. The moment is captured with innocence-shattering savage directness. Gurney recognises that it is language itself that is changed, fractured, left "half-witted". 'Glory' becomes a grinning death's-head in the gilt family frame; and the reality is in those nonsense words (one thinks of the scene in *Journey's End* where Osborne recites Lewis Carroll). What clinches this poem is the shift:

> But here, having escaped the steely showers
> Endured through panged intolerable hours
> The expensive and much determined doom,
> Find slow death in the loved street and bookish room.

It is not just a poem about the trenches at all, but about the aftermath and Gurney is speaking of the horror of survival, the "slow death in the loved street and bookish room".

It was slow death for Ivor Gurney. In 1918 he began to hear voices and wished to be sent to an asylum: he even sent Marion Scott a suicide note. Again it is hard to distinguish the visionary from the insane at such times. He responded to the world aurally; the hearing of voices and of all kinds of sounds is a key element in his poems and he even 'scores' them like pieces of music: the distant crying of the wounded man, then the brief 'close-up' exchange in 'The Silent One'; the crescendo of Welsh singers in 'First Time In'; the sudden clarinet playing "a hundred pipers" in 'Crucifix Corner'; the "thumping and grinding" of the guns. Even the sound of the wind on Witscombe Steep and the ominous "dark river voice below" in the last line of 'The Lock-Keeper'... But Gurney's state of mind was evidently not secure and he was discharged from the army in October. The immediate post-war months were an unsettled period for many men, but Gurney seemed particularly affected and found it difficult to settle back to his musical studies with Vaughan Williams. He spent much time night-walking, shifting from job to job, frequently cadging, becoming a burden on his family. He found moments of tranquillity, as when he occupied an empty farmhouse under Crickley Hill. And he was still writing, having books published (*War's Embers*, 1919) and acquiring something of a reputation – not always of the right kind.

1919-22 is usually considered the period of Ivor Gurney's finest work, when he learned to tighten and control, but also to exploit the "queerness" so as to release new possibilities. Not all of his writing concerns the war – such major pieces as 'The Lock-Keeper', 'Felling a Tree' or 'Cotswold Ways' come from this period – but there are some of his best accounts of everyday trench life: 'Billet', for example or the wonderful eight lines of 'After War'. Some of the best have long remained uncollected: 'Half Dead', 'Riez Bailleul Also' or 'Trees Over There'. Particularly interesting are poems which read like scrapbooks or journals of war memory. 'Laventie' is a good example, and those about battle itself, such as the first poem called 'Near Vermand', which begins: "Lying flat on my belly shivering in clutch-frost,/There was time to watch the stars, we had dug in ..." This shows Gurney's ability to suggest obsessive nerve-grinding indignity of routine and misery. The language never settles into recognisable stable sentence forms, but shivers and crouches like the poet. Memories of home flash via parentheses ("Cotswold her spinnies if ever") inserted into the broken colloquial flow (" ... would be relieved/In a quarter or so") yet still the language keeps its spirits up with the playful note: "Worry in snow flurry". 'The Not-returning' is one of his most lyrical poems from this time and although it sounds rather like Hopkins, it compares interestingly with Edward Thomas' 'Lights Out'. Like his beloved Elizabethans, Gurney was intrigued by sleep, but this poem is evocative too of war's camaraderie rather than its horror: the paradoxical pleasures of weariness in a close community. The "not-returning" is no lament for missing soldiers, but for the the poet himself and a lost way of life. 'Lovely Playthings' is another important poem from 1919-22, a short intense lyric which contrasts the effect on the spirit of sunrise and sunset and neatly captures the swinging moods in Ivor Gurney himself: the surge of sunrise optimism and the blind battle with hopelessness at day's end. Life is portrayed as a series of dawns and dusks with nothing much in between, where day is "admitted", like some guilty truth.

Dawn is one of the Great War's great themes, as Paul Fussell has shown. It is also one of Gurney's key words, of which there are many. The way in which he refuses to drop certain words or themes has been put down to his mental condition, but they certainly become recognisable landmarks in his poetry. "Dawn" (three times in 'Lovely

Playthings'), "hill", "stars", "west", "steep", "tired", "clean", "square" ("each square joy's hour" in 'By Severn') as opposed to "curve" (see "When from the curve ..."), "chance" ("chance of line", "chance of death"), "mist" and of course "thing". There are others; but Ivor Gurney can always produce the unexpected word too and as he matures in his writing he learns to avoid the obvious. Not for him the poppies; he prefers to highlight the cabbages (see 'Robecq Again'). He says in 'The Escape' that he believes in "whatever/leads to the seeing of small trifles" and one poem he titles 'The Dearness of Common Things'.

Yet what is common to Ivor Gurney is not only "tea, plate, shelves" but also Schubert, Beethoven, Dürer, Whitman, Drummond of Hawthornden, Ben Jonson. He is not a literary writer like Edmund Blunden, but literature is part of the furniture around him. He sees Canadian troops and thinks of Jack London. He remembers England in terms of her authors in 'I Saw England (July Night)'. The titles alone – particularly of his later poems – suggest what presences furnished his mind with solace and meaning in the darkest hours of the asylum. Voices were speaking and singing to him, but he also found himself taking on their personalities, as in the Whitmanesque last poem of *Collected Poems*, 'As They Draw to a Close'.

There was a deterioration in Gurney's condition after the unsettled year of 1922, when he lost several jobs – cinema organist, farm labourer – and planted himself uninvited on his brother. After several suicide attempts he was eventually certified insane and admitted on 28th September to Barnwood House asylum near Gloucester, then just before Christmas to the City of London Mental Hospital, Dartford ('Stone House') where he remained until his death. Over the next 15 years he worked obsessively on his collections of songs and poems, while fighting off bouts of insanity. Some of the writings from this time are heartbreaking – witness, the letter to the police quoted at the beginning of Michael Hurd's biography, with its paranoia about electricity.

His powers as a poet waned, but no more than any other poet in his middle years and there are fine things from the last period. In his final months a symposium of his work was prepared in the influential *Music and Letters*, but although a copy was rushed to him on its publication, he was too weak to appreciate its significance. The movement to proclaim him not only as a significant composer but as the 'War Poet' he always believed himself to be was already under way, even as he died on Boxing Day 1937.

Further Reading and Listening

Gurney:
Collected Poems (ed. P..J. Kavanagh, Carcanet, revised edition, 2004)
Selected Poems (ed. Walter, Everyman 1996)
Rewards of Wonder (ed. Walter, Carcanet, 2000)
Collected Letters (ed. Thornton, Carcanet, 1995)

* * *

Bostridge, Ian, *The English Songbook* (EMI, 1999)
Hurd, Michael, *The Ordeal of Ivor Gurney* (OUP, 1978)
Lucas, John, *Ivor Gurney* (Northcote House, 2001)
Lucas, John, *Starting to Explain* (Trent Books, 2003)
Parker, Rennie, *Ivor Gurney – an Introduction* (The Gurney Society, 2004)
Partridge, Ian, *Songs by Gurney and Delius* (Etcetera, 1989)

4

Laurence Binyon 1869-1943

The British Library recently issued a rare, undated recording taken from a Japanese 78rpm disc, of Laurence Binyon reading 'For the Fallen'. It is extraordinary to hear the voice of the creator of this iconic poem: pronouncing its title, *"For the Fall-in"*, then proceeding to intone with a Yeatsian quaver in his voice, at a lugubrious pace, and most portentously: "With proud thanksgiving, a mother for her child-*rin*,/England mourns for her dead across the sea ... " A portent this poem certainly was: 'For the Fallen', the archetypal poem of remembrance, was composed in September 1914, just after the retreat from Mons, when the war had barely begun; the weight of grief and knowing gloom that we hear in Binyon's recorded voice is, much of it, retrospective. The words themselves, however, are charged with the preoccupations and abstract heroics of the hour; any ambiguities – those echoes of soldier Enobarbus' description of the duplicitous Cleopatra in the famous fourth stanza – are surely unconscious. England is Victoria, Britannia, and Shakespeare's Elizabeth: a feminine power, maternal, protective, proud. We are not meant to think of Actium.

That Binyon was able to strike such an enduring elegiac note at that moment in 1914 was perhaps because he was already in his mid-40s when war broke out: the eldest of all the poets highlighted here. It does not, of course, explain his uncanny prescience in choosing "the going down of the sun and in the morning", times which were to be crucial in trench ritual, and in anticipating the profound need for a poem adequate to the aftermath. Nevertheless, the Boer War, even the Crimean War, would have meant more to him than to many of those young men who joined up. He had had a lifetime in which to ponder human conflict, and although he was hardly involved in the war effort when he wrote 'For the Fallen' (he was Curator of the Oriental prints and paintings in the British Museum from 1913-1933) he did later "see action". He used his annual leave to volunteer from July-September 1915 and again in 1916 as a Red Cross Orderly, based in a hospital in Arc-en-Barrois in the Marne, tending to French casualties. As a literary figure of some reputation, he had also come to know promising young poets who were leaving for the Front – Isaac Rosenberg, for example, who had sent him verses to consider in 1912 (he eventually wrote the introduction to Rosenberg's *Selected Poems* in 1922). Binyon's age endows his verse with some authority and enables him to adopt an occasionally paternalistic stance (in for example, 'The Unreturning Spring'), to see the wider picture and to feel the loss of so much potential. None of the younger poets here would have been moved to write 'Oxford in War-time', a poem which gives voice to the gradual public realisation that an entire generation was being wiped out, that England – win or lose – would never be the same country.

(Robert) Laurence Binyon was born on 10th August (St Laurence's Day) in Lancaster. His family were of Quaker stock and had strong Welsh roots, the name Binyon deriving from the Welsh *Ap Einion*. From an early age, Laurence was passionate about drawing and writing poetry. At St Paul's, Hammersmith, where he was educated, he was nicknamed "the Bard", but it was here that he made an important friend in Manmohan Ghose, an Indian boy whose views on spirituality had a lasting effect on him, encouraging his scepticism towards organised religion, and his fascination with Zen and Tao. At Trinity College Oxford, where he won the Newdigate Prize, he began to move in literary and artistic circles, meeting Robert Bridges, who read to him from manuscripts of Gerard Manley Hopkins. He went on to become a considerable authority on Oriental culture, lecturing in Japan between the wars, and his books on Chinese art are still well respected – as are his influential studies of British artists such as Palmer and Blake. In April 1904 he married Cicely Powell, who had walked through his Print Room door like Dante's vision of Beatrice. Her wealthy family regarded young Laurence as something of a Bohemian and were shocked by how little he earned, but the shock was reciprocated when, just after the birth of their twin daughters, Cicely's father died and it was revealed that he was deeply in debt.

Despite Binyon's enormous reputation in the field of print expertise, money problems were never far away in their household, especially in the years leading up to the war, when a third daughter was born. Matters were not helped by Binyon's increasingly anti-materialistic views. Following the publication of his two volume *Collected Poems* in 1931, after his retirement from the staff of the Museum, he became Norton Professor of Poetry at Harvard, then Byron Professor at the University of Athens. There was a Faber collection, *The North Star*, in 1941. The last decade of his life was devoted to translating Dante into English *terza rima* and to cultivating fruit trees – a reaction to the devastation he saw in the orchards of France during his visits to the Western Front. Laurence Binyon died on 10th March 1943 and is buried in Aldworth churchyard, Berkshire.

Binyon is the most quoted and least well known of the war poets we are considering here. This is partly to do with the overshadowing success of 'For the Fallen' and partly that Binyon's war poetry is hidden in the depths of his long out-of-print *Collected Poems* and there has never been a *Selected*. Even a biography had to wait 50 years: he had discouraged those who wished to write one and Cicely herself never produced the promised memoir. Yet Grierson and Smith, in *A Critical History of English Poetry,* suggest that Binyon was "the poet on whom the war produced the most remarkable effect ... His voice took on a deeper note; his verse broke into larger and more turbulent rhythms. He wrote, always in the same exalted strain, of the things he had seen with his own eyes". This is generally true. It is also unsurprising. As John Hatcher's biography states – he worked 13 hours a day:

> ... hefting them on to stretchers and sometimes beds up and down the winding stairs ... rooms to be fumigated, clothes and blankets disinfected ... sand collected for sandbags, windows cleaned, stores shifted, meals served, wine brought up from cellars.

He had to swab suppurating patients and incinerate amputated limbs. While hardly like life in the trenches, it was a gruelling experience for someone of such a sheltered background. While his war work was entirely in France, he had always had a special affection for another part of the Front. Before the war, he had travelled to

Belgium several times and published in 1899 his book *Western Flanders*, a collection of prose meditations, in which he calls Ypres "impregnable to the agitations of this modern age". His prescience could not always be relied upon.

Yet one of the reasons for his neglect is that Binyon remains for much of the time the unashamed Victorian in his attitude to war. 'The Fourth of August' begins:

Now in thy splendour go before us,
Spirit of England, ardent-eyed,
Enkindle this dear earth that bore us,
In the hour of peril purified.

Following the conventional wisdom of the early years of the war, this poem speaks of purging and winnowing, (*The Winnowing-Fan* is the title of his wartime slim volume) although the poet also acknowledges the "barren creed of blood and iron", which was not a common view at this stage.

What is interesting to the modern reader, however, is the way Binyon's war poetry – particularly the work inspired by his stretcher-bearing work in France – veers closer to the style of better known 'trench poets', only to swerve back to what he feels comfortable with. As John Hatcher writes: "the full horror of this hospital overflowing with victims of … the most brutal battle in history is kept from his poetry. Binyon just did not have the vocabulary." But in, for example, 'Ebb of War' and here in 'Fetching the Wounded', the broken rhythms, the restless punctuation, the plain-spoken business-like tone of the piece, suggest that the poet has been shaken to within a semi-colon of Modernism:

… we bring
Stretchers, and pile and number them; and heap
The blankets ready. Then we wait and keep
A listening ear. Nothing comes yet; all's still,
Only soft gusts upon the wires blow shrill
Fitfully, with a gentle spot of rain …

Could anything be more different from 'For the Fallen'? That "listening ear" might well have hoped to hear a fellow lyric poet. It is the death of a style:

... trembling poplars and lamp-whitened grass,
A brief procession flitting like a thought
Through a brain drowsing into slumber; nought
But we awake in the solitude immense!

Binyon is troubled, though not troubled at the deeper level as, say, Blunden was: but Blunden was only in his late teens when he found himself on the Somme. Even Binyon's last great masterpiece, the poem 'The Burning of the Leaves' (from the posthumous collection of that title) shrewdly picked out by Philip Larkin for his Oxford anthology, shows him facing a second world war, and singing of "stripping the spirit bare", but not quite able to do it. "Stubborn stalks crackle as they resist", but he goes on tending his bonfire and will not speak out. There is no 'Report on Experience' like Blunden's. No 'Have you forgotten yet?' like Sassoon. Instead, the tight-lipped monosyllables as he burns up past "rootless hopes and fruitless desire":

Let them go to the fire, with never a look behind.
The world that was ours is a world that is ours no more.

Binyon has much in common with Elgar, with whom he corresponded, begging that he (rather than the less well known Cyril Rootham) should set 'For the Fallen' to music:

... think of England, of the English-speaking peoples, in whom the common blood stirs now as it never did before; think of the awful casualty lists that are coming, & the losses in more & more homes; think of the thousands who will be craving to have their grief glorified & lifted up & transformed by an art like yours ...   (27th March 1915)

Elgar was swayed by the poet's self-serving rhetoric, and his composition, *The Spirit of England*, sets three of Binyon's war poems to music: it is considered by Elgar's biographer, Jerrold Northrop Moore, to be "his finest music since the Second Symphony". The settings led to further collaborations, including music for Binyon's verse play about King Arthur, which has recently found new life in Anthony Payne's hugely popular reconstruction of the unfinished Third Symphony. Binyon would surely have approved and would have appreciated too the 'skeletal' quality in Payne's 'elaborations'. Both Binyon and Elgar had a growing desire in their latter years to escape the pre-war gestures, to achieve a spareness of style which was yet adequate to the depths of despair they felt. 'The Burning of the Leaves' could be said to be Binyon's cello concerto. Even in late summer 1914, as Binyon was in Cornwall writing "They shall grow not old", T.S. Eliot had put in his own bid for immortality with "I grow old ... I grow old ..." By the time Eliot's 'Prufrock' appeared, in 1917, its French dedicatee was dead in the Dardanelles and America was joining the war. But on the poetic front, her voice was already 'over here' and growing louder. In one of his letters, Eliot describes how in November 1919 he gave a lecture on 'Modern Techniques in Poetry', chaired by the 50-year-old Laurence Binyon: "a middle-aged poetic celebrity who evidently knew nothing about me except that I was supposed to be the latest rage, and he didn't understand it and didn't like it". Yet Eliot and Binyon held in common a deep repugnance towards materialism and a horror of the new age's vulgarity and barrenness. Binyon's 40-page poem, 'The Idols' was a great hit when it appeared in 1928, but perhaps not with the same readers who had acclaimed 'The Waste Land' six years earlier. Eliot came to admire Binyon's later work (particularly his late poem 'In Hospital') and even published a collection at Faber. Binyon in turn learnt to respect Eliot, hearing in 'The Waste Land' the "jangled music" of "a remarkable poem".

But Binyon's celebrity would not endure, and for all his authority and gravity on the British Library CD, he already sounds like a lost soul. Lines from 'For the Fallen', engraved (without acknowledgement) and still to be seen at the entrance to the British Museum, his workplace for 40 years, are prophetic in more ways than he knew when he wrote them. His poem has become an anonymous artefact, like the Rosetta Stone. In later portraits Binyon looks a touch self-pitying, as if he has discovered that what he prophesied is happening: he has "grown old", no edition of his verse available, only remembered for Remembrance's sake (but more often the poem is unattributed) or somewhere in the origins of a melody on an Elgar disc, or in the guise of translator. His fine version of Dante's *The Divine Comedy* is certainly not quite forgotten yet. Ezra Pound, who knew Binyon fairly well and christened him "BinBin", called it "the most interesting English version ... that I have seen or expect to see" and wrote an extended essay on its strengths. What he also noted was that the experience of translating Dante had purged Binyon of his excesses, of what he called the poison in "the abominable dog-biscuit of Milton's rhetoric".

The war poems deserve to be known, although plenty of them taste rather of Pound's dog-biscuit. They express much faith in the healing power of Earth and there is plenty of jingoistic packaging, but Binyon often surprises us in the 60 pages of *Collected Poems* devoted to his war poetry: his devotion to the spiritual values of the east seeps in from time to time, and it is not quite true (as Grierson and Smith suggested) that he is relentlessly "exalted". These poems read well as a cycle, varied in their metres and stanza-forms (ballad, narrative, sonnet), some smacking of Hardy, some of Whitman, developing from the patriotic indulgence of 'The Fourth of August', through the poet's experience of ambulance duty, to reflective pieces 'in memoriam'. A particular surprise comes towards the end of the sequence, in his bitter attack on the "dissolving littleness" of the peacetime society to which the soldiers return, although one can see that Binyon's taste for Zen and Tao would not find much advocacy in the Roaring Twenties. Among the shorter poems, I would recommend to any reader or would-be anthologist (in the order they appear) 'The Healers', which avoids abstraction by personifying the guidance we might find in Goethe's "eternal feminine": one cannot help but think of those touchstones of Victorian piety, Florence Nightingale and 'The Light of the World'. 'The Zeppelin' is a memorable poem, where the 'elation' of an attack on the Home Front stirs in the poet a new energy and immediacy, partly no doubt because of his own hatred of what he called "property feeling" and the "sentiment of ownership". Perhaps his finest achievement is 'The Ebb of War', which follows 'Fetching the Wounded' in *Collected Poems,* and shares its broken rhythms:

> All is as it was
> At the instant of the shattering: flat-thrown walls;
> Dislocated rafters; lintels blown awry
> And toppling over; what were windows, mere
> Gapings on mounds of dust and shapelessness ...

In some of the detail there is the sense of despised bourgeois conventions and complacencies being overturned: "a limp bell-pull; here and there/Little printed papers pasted on the wall./It is like a madness crumpled up in stone". But elsewhere the imperial bell-note still sounds. He cannot resist writing of "myriads", for example, a word that he frequently resorts to and one which suggests the struggle he has to see clearly what is before him. No one could look at the Thiepval memorial and think "a myriad hearts". Nevertheless, there is considerable 'reportage' here and the art historian describes faithfully when he can bring himself to look. When he does look – at Zeppelin, wounded man, or bombed house – Binyon is equal to the task. Like the Chinese poets he admired and translated, he super-imposes very precisely drawn vignettes against an atmospheric inky wash.

'Mid Atlantic' is the embodiment of this style: the ocean liner sketched on a vast, threatening sea. "Elemental" was a favourite word of Binyon's, "rhythm" was another. The sea suggests both, together with the Buddhist (and, it has to be said, Wordsworthian) feeling of "the continuity of the universe" (*Painting in the Far East,* 1908). The ship was in fact the *Lusitania,* some five months before she was torpedoed. Whether or not the premonitory mood was in the poem from the start (Binyon claims to have written it on board), it is a powerful poem: "If this were all! – A dream of dread/Ran through me; I watched the waves that fled/Pale-crested out of hollows black,/ The hungry lift of helpless waves,/A million million tossing graves ..." It would not be the first time that he had anticipated the future.

Other poems worth discovering are 'La Patrie', from his second tour, and 'Morn Like a Thousand Shining Spears' – two of the many contemporary responses to dawn and birdsong about which Paul Fussell has written so fascinatingly in *The Great War and Modern Memory.* The latter lyric sees day as the invader. It is fairly conventional in its *aabb* quatrains, as is 'The Sower (Eastern France)', which follows Hardy in his faith that "this will go onward the same/ Though Dynasties pass", that certain roads will always be trodden, whether by "creaking wain" or "a battery ... with horses and guns". The lingering second line suggests a gloomy faith in the future and there are many striking touches: that grim ringing of the harness shows again how sounds were so important to poets of this war;

then, "the guns with mouths declined" echoed later in a painterly manner by the farmer "sowing his children's bread" ; and a lovely detail about a sun-dried furrow:

> Familiar, year by year, to the creaking wain
> Is the long road's level ridge above the plain.
> Today a battery comes with horses and guns
> On the straight road, that under the poplars runs,
> At leisurely pace, the guns with mouths declined,
> Harness merrily ringing ...

Where the rhyme and metre are reassuringly conventional here, elsewhere they are ambitious and unexpected. The aggressive trochaics of 'Guns at the Front', for instance, a poem written during his third visit to France in 1917, when the Red Cross had asked him to travel through France and report on the work of volunteers: "Monsters roaring aloud with hideous vastness,/*Nothing, Nothing, Nothing!* And man that made them/Mightier far than himself, has stooped, and obeyed them ..." Binyon's metres begin to challenge his own belief in unbreakable inherited patterns. 'Hunger' has a very direct, modern, bare-bones texture, whose riddling note seems to hark back to the Anglo-Saxons: "I come among the peoples like a shadow./I sit down by each man's side.//None sees me, but they look on one another,/And know that I am there".

Undoubtedly, a change comes over Binyon by the end of the war: "There is a newness in the world begun/A difference in the setting of the sun". But the sun goes on setting in its Edwardian way as his work moves into the 1920s. The radical thinking is not in his poetry but in his letters and writings on the art of the east, where he anticipates our own environmental concerns in recommending "beauty cherished for its own sake, not for its use and service in the life of man" (*Painting in the Far East*). Squeezed in towards the very end of his wartime selection, however, is one striking poem which we should not overlook. It was written after he had been sent to France in mid-October 1918 to join the Allied advance – not to tend to casualties this time, not to write reports, certainly not to fight. Rather, to give the troops a series of lectures on Chinese civilisation! 'An Incident at Cambrai' is notable because it brings to the fore Binyon's love for and professional expertise concerning Oriental culture and for a moment the individuality of the poet shines through. There are not many figures in Binyon's war-torn landscapes as a rule, and ironically the appeal of Chinese art to him was the unimportance of personality: man and nature blend into one spiritual whole. But in this poem he sees Chinese workmen clearing the ruins in Cambrai and we are reminded that here was, after all, a 'world' war. He successfully juggles the traditional lyric and ballad virtues, the conventional inversions and poeticisms, with tricks learnt from Arthur Waley, Ezra Pound and certain Chinese poets; and he introduces a harder, more rough-edged style, employing alliteration and as bold a word as 'rubble' in the opening line:

> In a by-street, blocked with rubble
> And any-way-tumbled stones,
> Between the upstanding house-fronts'
> Naked and scorched bones,
>
> Chinese workmen were clearing
> The ruins, dusty and arid.
> Dust whitened the motley coats,
> Where each his burden carried.

Again it is the sound that catches the poet's attention: a "solitary reaper", or a "nightingale" for this post-Romantic waste land. Among the silent workers, one sings "a high, sad, half-choked ditty":

> Was it love, was it grief, that made
> For long-dead lips that song?
> The desolation of Han
> Or the Never-Ending Wrong?

It is as if when everything to be seen has been destroyed, all that is left is what the ears can pick out – which is perhaps why Laurence Binyon's voice rings out so poignantly, so startlingly, from that Far Eastern shellac disc.

Further Reading

Binyon:
Collected Poems Vol 1: Lyrical Poems (Macmillan, 1931)
The Burning of the Leaves and Other Poems (London, 1944)
The North Star and Other Poems (Faber, 1941)
Painting in the Far East (London, 1908)

* * *

Hatcher, John, *Laurence Binyon: Poet, Scholar of East and West* (Clarendon, 1996)
Moore, Jerrold, Northrop, *Edward Elgar: a creative life* (OUP, 1984)
Pound, Ezra, *Literary Essays of Ezra Pound* (Faber, 1954)

5

Edmund Blunden 1896-1974

Edmund Blunden was the youngest of the major poets to find themselves at the Front. Only 18 when the war began, he had just left his beloved Christ's Hospital and could have taken up a classics scholarship to Oxford, but chose to volunteer for the Royal Sussex Regiment in 1915. Even then "he lived for poetry" (as one of his teachers put it) and had already seen a book of his work in print. It would be hard to overstate the significance of these tranquil early years, when he began his love affair with the countryside, a love that would survive everything the Great War could hurl at it. Within months of joining up, this young man from Kent found himself in the Somme, and having survived that, he was transferred to Ypres in time for Passchendaele and "a whole sweet countryside amuck with murder". It is remarkable that he came through at all, let alone with his sanity and a quiet religious instinct intact. Perhaps it is that very sanity, that modest spirituality, that tendency to write of 'undertones' rather than the immediate drama that has made him one of the most neglected masters among the war poets. But more probably it is his extraordinarily archaic style.

Opening a book of Blunden's verse is like stepping into the time of William Collins and Thomas Gray. It is as if Ezra Pound had never existed, as if Elizabeth Barrett Browning and Clough and all the other Victorian stylistic purists had never happened. He can make Wordsworth himself, with his "very language of men", sound modern. Many readers (until recently, myself among them) have found that they simply did not know how to read what can seem like a parody of the late Augustans. For Grierson and Smith in their landmark history of English poetry he was just stodgy. But to write off Blunden on these grounds would be as foolish as to reject Stravinsky because his neo-classical style was cold or to object to Peter Maxwell Davies writing string quartets because the genre is outdated: artists choose the way of writing which can best express their feelings. If the old sounds can be revivified, recast under new pressures, then they must be heard. When Spenser wrote 'The Faerie Queen', he was deliberately choosing an archaic style. Tennyson, too, knew there were other ways of writing 'Idylls of the King'. Pound himself adopted archaic mannerisms, but appeared less "out of key with his time" because he had broken the pentameter. Blunden uses the old metres: blank verse and sonnet, the Spenserian stanza and the ballad. He keeps a tight hold on the 18th century baby and will not throw out its bathwater: inversions and elisions, apostrophe and personification, together with an abundance of literary references. He reserves the right to use all these things. But when he chooses to, Blunden can write as purely and plainly as Edward Thomas and with as much colloquial passion as Sassoon and with a richness and depth rivalled only by Owen.

Yet, it is sometimes as if the war that shaped Blunden was a war fought not only for England but for English poetic style. Keats himself becomes a victim, as in the opening of 'Vlamertinghe: Passing the Chateau, July, 1917', a metrically shattered poem which yet remains as much a sonnet as those stumps on the Somme remain trees, and which quotes 'Ode on a Grecian Urn', remarking ominously: "But we are coming to the sacrifice". And in 'Preparations for Victory', it is Keats' garden, surely, that we are in: "there mossed boughs are hung/With apples whose bright cheeks none might excel,/And [t]here's a house as yet unshattered by a shell". In no other poet of the First World War, except perhaps David Jones, does this question of style become such an issue. Elsewhere, Blunden steps into the metrical shoes of other poets, most effectively in 'Rural Economy', which takes William Cowper's metre from 'The Castaway' and creates (as Paul Fussell points out) "an inverted, sardonic pastoral appropriate to the new kind of 'harvest' being reaped in France". Blunden is doing here what Eliot would do in his own way in 'The Waste Land', with its parodies of Spenser, Shakespeare, Pope and others. Blunden is no parodist (though some later 'tributes' come close, as this for Collins: "If aught of native verse in far-off years/ May hope, O pensive soul ...") but he certainly anticipates Joseph

Brodsky's conviction that metres are "sacred vessels" in which the verities of poetic truth are handed down through the ages from poet to poet.

Blunden is a writer of no less sophistication than Jones or Eliot and just because he is not labelled a 'Modernist' but a 'Georgian' it does not mean that he is going to ignore a resource. Blunden the poet was as resourceful as Blunden the soldier – and may in time prove to be just as much a survivor. He knows, for example, that juxtaposition must be the abiding stylistic feature of 1914-18, and that it is effective to use his natural grand style and then follow it with something much simpler, as in the first four lines of 'The Zonnebeke Road', where an ironic William Collins manner gives way to a line out of 'In Memoriam':

> Morning, if this late withered light can claim
> Some kindred with that merry flame
> Which the young day was wont to fling through space!
> Agony stares from each gray face.

But what becomes increasingly absorbing as one reads Blunden's work is his ability (learnt, perhaps, from John Clare) to give a physicality and a precision to the most elaborate of lines. Here, Pound would be pleased to note, is no "dim land of peace". Instead, we have the trenches of war, metrical zigzags, lit by the harsh lights of rhyme, and busy with the real "language of men":

> Why, see old Stevens there, that iron man,
> Melting the ice to shave his grotesque chin:
> Go ask him, shall we win?
> I never liked this bay, some foolish fear
> Caught me the first time that I came in here;
> That dugout fallen in awakes, perhaps,
> Some formless haunting of some corpse's chaps.

There is really nothing archaic about this, except his choice of "chaps", which is needed to make us think briefly, with a dark smile, of the jester, Yorrick. Jon Silkin says of this passage that "Blunden creates a brilliantly knowing and bitter facetiousness", although there is nothing of Sassoon's corrosive sarcasm. Sassoon would have been more likely to use "chaps" in the modern slang sense: "'Poor young chap,'/I'd say – 'I used to know his father well'". Blunden's view of things is more like Hamlet's, the shrapnel is lodged more deeply. His experience does not easily convert to humour and even less easily to anger. It pollutes and infects so that all his post-war poetry is to some extent 'about' the war, even though the titles do not necessarily suggest it; ("The titles and contents of my books" he wrote, "have labelled me among the poets of the time as a useful rustic"). Sassoon's limitation as a poet is that he never became a poet of the language itself, his obsessions drove him to use words, not to crawl into them. Blunden is more vulnerable, does not wear Sassoon's armour; his only protection is nature and the tradition of poetry itself. War becomes a pike in a mill-race or a sudden vague shadow in his later life like "a shark in a sandy bay" ('Long Moments'); most memorably it is there under the ice and frozen into the very diction of 'Midnight Skaters':

> With but a crystal parapet
> Between, he has his engines set.

It is interesting that in a recorded interview from 1964 (in *The Poet's Voice* series), asked about what inspired his poetry, he said "I think something quite accidental disturbs something else. It's like digging in the sand and hitting a remaining landmine". That word "disturbs" is one he comes back to; it is revealing.

But in the wider context of his *Poems of Many Years*, war only occasionally rises to the surface. Those poems where war is undoubtedly the 'subject' become consequently all the more important. Blunden's prose memoir, *Undertones of War*, is as aptly titled as Graves' breezy *Goodbye To All That* – the one a piece of theatre, with Graves in the hero's role, the former an accurate but largely dispassionate account in which the "young shepherd in a soldier's coat" is always lurking in the shadows – something Lieutenant Edmund Blunden, MC certainly did not do. He chose to append a substantial group of his war poems to this memoir and this is still the most easily acquired introduction to the poetry. The selection includes his greatest poem of the war, 'Third Ypres', which I now wish to discuss.

John H. Johnston, in his helpful chapter on Blunden in *English Poetry of the First World War* compares the prose account of an incident as given in *Undertones of War* with the same occasion described in 'Third Ypres' and remarks that there is not "the slightest hint of his own feelings and sensations ... [his] experience is one with the objective physical context and falls into place amid the succession of incidents which make up the narrative action". But the poem is a different matter. It is a boldly constructed work of art in which Blunden pushes himself to the limits and the cracks in his Georgian manners open up in a thrillingly dramatic way.

The title 'Third Ypres' is shorthand for the third 'Battle' of Ypres, which culminated in the mud- and blood-bath of Passchendaele. Having come through the fighting on the Somme around Thiepval, an experience commemorated in several essential poems – notably, 'Thiepval Wood' and 'Two Voices' – Blunden's battalion was moved to the notorious Ypres Salient, the poet himself managing to squeeze in a brief visit home before renewing his acquaintance with the battlefield. He was gassed twice, in July and October of 1917. 'Third Ypres' was, like many of his best poems, written "in tranquillity" some years after the war. It is at least as ambitious as Owen's 'Dulce Et Decorum Est ' and 'Strange Meeting', displaying a maturity of scope and expression that those who died on the Front hardly had time to emulate. For all his experiments with half-rhyme and resonant mythologies, Owen did not venture this far into the avant-garde. Blunden's poem is almost like a Cubist painting, glimpsing its subject from contrasting angles. In its cutting and panning techniques, it anticipates the cinematic style of Modernism. But its metre is thoroughly traditional. He uses blank verse, letting rhyme go with a shrug of inevitability reminiscent of the loss of his grandfather's "ebony walking-stick" in the opening pages of *Undertones*: "It went. I was away from it only a few minutes – it went". Metre Blunden never abandons: it is more than a walking-stick, it is his orders from HQ.

The 'undertones' in this poem are of Nature inverted, corrupted, perverted: like Nature in *Macbeth* or *Julius Caesar*. Blunden is not the only poet to compare barbed wire to the hawthorn hedges of home, although it is typical that he should say "an unplashed hedge" incorporating both a dialect word worthy of Clare and a precise point of agricultural order. We certainly feel that here is a poet who is attuned to the world beyond his study, to subtle changes in the weather when he writes "Now dulls the day and chills" or "then the sky's/ Mute misery lapses into trickling rain,/That wreathes and swims and soon shuts in our world", but the weather at 'Wipers' was hardly subtle. "The grey rain ... the shrouding rain ... still wept the rain ..." The death of an individual is of much less moment: "He's gone,/ Falls on a knee ... Well I like[d] him, that young runner,/But there's no time for that". In a less literary, less bucolic poet it might come across as tasteless to comment on natural history in such circumstances. The fine poem, 'Illusions', explores this ambiguity and the difficulty in seeing "dancing dewy grasses" or hearing "the brave bird/In the sighing orchard" alongside "Death's malkins dangling in the wire". In a poem about Passchendaele, scene of the slaughter of 400,000 men, Blunden still manages to turn our attention to details of the environment. Like John Clare, he does not look away, does not moralise, does not make an abstraction of a physical reality, even if he uses a literary reference to intensify it (and why not, since this was the most literary army in history?) And it was, after all, the local environment, its mud and wind and frost, that most preoccupied the men themselves, as Owen's 'Exposure' reminds us. At the climax of 'Third Ypres', after a series of numbing horrors, "the churn of moonless night and mud/And flaming burst and sour gas ... huge and shattering salvoes", the poet's pill-box is struck. The actual strike is described in a manner curiously and, one presumes, realistically dream-like ("dream" is, of course, a favourite Blunden word):

> The demon grins to see the game, a moment
> Passes, and – still the drum-tap dongs my brain
> To a whirring void – through the great breach above me
> The light comes in with icy shock and the rain
> Horridly drips.

This is from the 1982 Carcanet edition, but variant versions of the passage have "horribly drips" and "horridly drops". I have suggested that Blunden is a poet who inhabits the language and here, in this incident which haunts him for the rest of his life, he desperately cries for words: "Doctor, talk, talk!", but the healer is "dead/Or stunned" and cannot grant him any means of expression, of exorcising the horror. All the poet can do is go on being a soldier ("March, sing, roar", as he says in 'Warning to Troops') and try and save his friends:

> ... O I'll drag you, friends,
> Out of the sepulchre into the light of day:
> For this is day, the pure and sacred day,
> And while I squeak and gibber over you,
> Out of [or Look, from] the wreck a score of field-mice nimble,
> And tame and curious look about them; (these
> Calmed me, on these depended my salvation).

Blunden begins to write in the fractured bell-notes of Ivor Gurney here, coming close to madness ("mad" is another of his key words). Some critics have found the mice an unsuccessful touch, suggesting that "his range of reference diminishes" so that the poem "does not fulfil its original narrative promise" (Johnston); but the point is that conventional narrative becomes impossible, the mice are the only small hope of salvation like the maddening "silver bird" of goodness in one of his ballads and he is reduced to squeaking like them. Silkin is more enthusiastic, noting that Blunden "uses all the means at his disposal both to express the terror and control it" and demonstrating how the pentameter operates in the third of the lines quoted above: "beautifully rounded and regular", making "both a positive statement and an attempt at reassurance". Silkin is an excellent guide to the metrical intricacies of Blunden's poem and it is important to realise just how central these are to its success.

Each line of his blank verse moves us forward, yet there are ceaseless shifts of tone, suggesting the surges of adrenalin, optimism, terror, cynicism, boredom, hopelessness. There is also a kaleidoscope of effects, from the uncertainty in the pauses of "No, these, smiled faith" to the sibilant onomatopoeia of the bullets. The pentameter itself can lull us into a sense of normality ("Amazing quiet fell upon the waste") or prepare us for a trochaic shock with a nod towards Binyon's 'For the Fallen': "They move not back, they lie among the crews/Twisted ..."

> Amazing quiet fell upon the waste,
> Quiet intolerable to those who felt
> The hurrying batteries beyond the masking hills

For their new parley setting themselves in array
In crafty fourms unmapped.
                          No, these, smiled faith,
Are dumb for the reason of their overthrow.
They move not back, they lie among the crews
Twisted and choked, they'll never speak again.
Only the copse where once might stand a shrine
Still clacked and suddenly hissed its bullets by.
The War would end, the Line was on the move,
And at a bound the impassable was passed.
We lay and waited with extravagant joy.

The syntactical inversions, the personification of "faith" – surely
these lines are moribund? But read them aloud, trying to keep the
right tone in the voice for what is being hinted at ("They move not
back"; "The War would end") and they start to breathe. The apparent
archaisms then come to seem like a diversionary tactic. Those "crafty
fourms unmapped" that the silent guns might be redeploying into
are being suggested by the sinuousness of the syntax. Even that
unexpected 'u' in "fourm" is like a sinister new trench where whatever
"disturbs" Blunden is hiding ready to snipe. The lines vividly conjure
a sense of "death at watch" as it was under the frozen pond.

In Blunden, as in Shakespeare, there is always something new
happening, and although he is no dramatist, his poetry has latent
drama in the patterns it makes in the air. This is not, after all, the
abstraction for which Georgians were so often damned. He is
particularly attuned to the sounds of war. In description: "The ice-
bound throat gulps out a gargoyle shriek./The wretched wire before
the village line/Rattles like rusty brambles or dead bine ..." ('The
Zonnebeke Road') but also in the overheard snippets, as in 'Two
Voices', where an officer's casual "There's something in the air"
leaves the troops unnerved, and one of the men mutters: "We're going
South, man".

In 'La Quinque Rue' (originally published in 1928 in *Undertones*),
where the memory of a particular road haunts him, and he finds it
hard to imagine that normal farm life must now have returned, it is
the heart-wrenching and awful sounds that catch our attention more
even than the "forlorn effigies of farms besprawled": "the flute or
fiddle ... That battered drum, say why it clacks and brags ... Why

clink those spades ... I know those muttering groups ..." But this aural sensitivity is not something Blunden particularly prized in himself. He says in *The Poet Speaks*: "the sense I had was of *painting* rather than describing" and it is probably for what Silkin calls his "scrupulous precision" that many readers will return to his work. In later years he was responsible for the rehabilitation of John Clare and it is with that sharp-eyed miniaturist of hedgerows and dark moods that he should be compared.

Edmund Blunden had home leave after Passchendaele ("the most wicked 24 hours I have ever been through") but was back yet again in time for an attack at Gouzeaucourt, where he was in charge of a wiring party under appalling machine-gun fire. His health was breaking down, the gas having affected his asthma, and he was eventually obliged to abandon his men ("Scarce a simpler traitor ever!" he writes bitterly in 'Gouzeaucourt: The Deceitful Calm') to spend the final months of the war in England. He was demobbed in 1919, but personal tragedy followed soon after when his young daughter, Joy, died. She is the subject of several touching elegies.

The substantial remainder of Blunden's life was spent in the world of journalism and academia, chiefly the latter. He was at Oxford, living near Masefield and Graves, then in Tokyo as Professor of English Literature, and later in Hong Kong. Volumes of his poetry appeared at regular intervals, his reputation having been established with *The Waggoner and Other Poems* (1920) and *The Shepherd and Other Poems of Peace and War* (1922). There were at least another 20 collections to follow before his death in 1974, but the prose memoir *Undertones of War* was his greatest success: it had to be reprinted three times in December of 1928 alone! He edited and wrote books on Christopher Smart, John Keats, Henry Vaughan, William Collins, and others, but most notably about Percy Bysshe Shelley and John Clare. He can be said to have begun the revival in interest in Clare's work. He also helped introduce to the public poetry by his contemporaries from the war: Wilfred Owen and Ivor Gurney. He was awarded the Queen's Gold Medal for Poetry in 1957, just before the broadest selection of his work appeared, *Poems of Many Years*, chosen by Rupert Hart-Davis (a book long out of print, but not hard to find second-hand) and he was appointed Professor of Poetry at

Oxford from 1966-68. He retired to Long Melford, Suffolk, in 1964 and is buried there.

Michael Schmidt suggests (in *Fifty Modern British Poets*) that 'Report on Experience', from the 1929 collection *Near and Far*, is Blunden's finest achievement. There must be several contenders for this, but no one should overlook the great narratives and stanzaic retrospectives of warfare: 'Third Ypres', 'The Zonnebeke Road', 'Trench Raid near Hooge', 'Return of the Native', '1916 seen from 1921', 'Preparations for Victory', nor the many Hardyesque 'ballads' and Sassoon-like 'reports' on everyday life in the wars ('Pillbox', 'An Infantryman', 'Transport Up at Ypres', 'The Sentry's Mistake', 'Zero', 'The Welcome', 'Concert Party: Busseboom', 'Trench Nomenclature'); and the lyrics of personal optimism, desolation or irony ('In Festubert', 'Illusions', 'The Ancre at Hamel', 'At Senlis Once', 'The Watchers'). Then there are the sonnets ('The Unchangeable', 'Warning to Troops', 'Vlamertinghe') and the poems of remembrance ('La Quinque Rue', 'Flanders Now', 'Memorial, 1914-1918', 'Can you Remember?'). And there is that extraordinary translation from the 1950s of Eugène Manuel's 'Vision', an ingeniously rhymed *tour de force* which concludes Blunden's *Poems of Many Years:*

> It was winter, and day dying;
> The cannons had just stopped brawling and braying,
> All about in the graying
> You saw Frenchmen and Germans lying.

'Report on Experience', then, is just one among many. But it is a startlingly good poem. It takes several paces back from the Front and gives us an unexpected new perspective, one that stretches from the ripening lands of Auden way beyond as far as the Elizabethan demesnes of Raleigh and Gascoigne. The opening two stanzas show us the war as if through sharp new field-glasses, with a clarity that only distance and the finest craftsmanship can offer:

> I have been young, and now am not too old;
> And I have seen the righteous forsaken,
> His health, his honour and his quality taken.
> This is not what we were formerly told.

I have seen a green country, useful to the race,
Knocked silly with guns and mines, its villages vanished,
Even the last rat and the last kestrel banished –
God bless us all, this was peculiar grace.

Further Reading

Blunden:

Poems of Many Years (ed. Rupert Hart-Davies, Collins, 1957)

Selected Poems, (ed. Robyn Marsack, Carcanet, 1982)

Undertones of War (including supplement of 32 poems) (Penguin, 1982)

* * *

Johnston, John, H., *English Poetry of the First World War* (Princeton, 1964)

Leavis, F.R., *New Bearings in English Poetry* (Penguin, 1972)

Lehmann, John, *The English Poets of the First World War* (Thames and Hudson, 1981)

Orr, Peter, (ed.) *The Poet Speaks* (Routledge, 1966)

Schmidt, Michael, *Fifty Modern British Poets* (Pan, 1979)

Silkin, Jon, *Out of Battle* (Routledge and Kegan Paul, 1972)

7

Siegfried Sassoon 1886-1967

It is curious how history tends to group poets into pairs: Keats goes with Shelley, Wordsworth with Coleridge, Pound with Eliot, Frost with Thomas. Readers like the double-act and so Auden is packed off to Iceland with MacNeice, Armitage and Maxwell following sixty years later. Siegfried Sassoon is usually introduced after Wilfred Owen as the 'other' great poet of the First World War. That these two poets did meet, that the elder had a considerable influence on the younger, is really incidental except to the specialist or the reader of Pat Barker's *Regeneration* trilogy. For the ordinary reader, Owen and Sassoon make an ideal partnership, the one rich, brooding, Keatsian, inward-looking, yet expansive and rather heavy-handed with the humour; the other sharp and angry, armed with full rhyme, economical, topical, accessible and fiercely witty. Owen writes late romantic symphonic music; Sassoon tries to be Stravinsky. In fact, he even wrote a poem about *The Rite of Spring* as if he heard in it not the dancing of the sacrificial victim, but young men marching themselves to death. But Sassoon's iconoclastic, "tank-storms-theatre" instincts do not adapt well to the full orchestral treatment. His poems are really more like jazz, the best of them small scale, ensemble pieces, where a soloist can wail: *But he did for them both by his plan of attack.*

The most obvious difference between Owen and Sassoon is that the latter had the chance to grow into a mature writer. He survived the First War and the Second to become not only a celebrated peace campaigner and Labour activist, but a respected literary editor and writer of prose, including what is often thought to be his masterpiece, *Memoirs of an Infantry Officer.* He lived long enough to snub modernists, to dismiss the likes of Robert Lowell and to become a literary eminence of the kind he courted in his youth, "a man awaiting the Georgian counter-revolution" as Craig Raine puts it. He does not have a white stone at Arras or a name on the memorial at Thiepval; he has a grave in the cosy churchyard of Mells, Somerset, where he had become involved with a Roman Catholic religious community. Long before the war, Siegfried Sassoon was already well positioned to make a reputation as a writer. Born in Kent into a wealthy and artistic family who had moved from London, his doting mother chose to call him Siegfried because she was keen on Wagner; the name Sassoon is Jewish and the boy had early experience of the rituals and traditions of Sephardic Jews. His early years were spent at Weirleigh in Brenchley, Kent, in a house whose door had carved over it the prescient motto *Vero nihil verius (Nothing is truer than truth)*. The sculptor father's infidelities led to a separation when Siegfried was only three and his parents never spoke to each other again, although the boy and his brothers saw a good deal of Alfred before his early death from TB. What he could never forget was the determined obstinacy in his parents' refusal to negotiate. An early appreciation, perhaps, of the circumstances of war and of what 'No Man's Land' can signify. Siegfried drifted through his school years, loath to concentrate, frequently sick, happiest when out fishing or discovering the solitary pleasures of the countryside. Horses and hunting became an obsession, one we are less able to equate with innocence and prelapsarian goodness today, perhaps, but nevertheless movingly celebrated in *Memoirs of a Fox-Hunting Man*.

Soon, poetry was making its mark on him. In his reading and his thinking, he was becoming preoccupied with the transience of human experience and the mystery of death. In a predominantly female, predominantly adult environment, music became increasingly important to him and this would become one of the most potent and distinctive features in his war poetry. More than any of his contemporaries, Sassoon is able to suggest both the glaring irony and the mystical otherness of birdsong in the trenches. But he is also attuned to the depth of feeling in the popular songs and it seems appropriate that he was still living when the Theatre Workshop staged *Oh What a Lovely War!* One of his most memorable poems is 'Everyone Sang' (p144, *The War Poems*) composed after the war, teetering on the edge of sentimentality, but finally more expressive of the popular grief of Remembrance than Binyon's dark suit and poppy-wreath elegy, 'For the Fallen'. Beyond this, there is the 'Secret Music' (p162) that "no din this side of death can quell": a powerful and largely unsatisfied spiritual yearning. We may remember the accusations hurled at God in some of the battlefield poems, but there is never the stony nothingness that his master Thomas Hardy described. Sassoon's bird in 'Thrushes' may scorn man's confused craving for deity, but there seems more possibility of our learning from its hopeful song than there is in Hardy's 'Darkling Thrush' of 1900.

Siegfried Sassoon's life up to 1914 tacks and drifts. He has plenty of money, good connections, and a vague desire to write. He opts first for Law then History at Cambridge, but neither is a priority, although he enjoys tutorials with William Morris, and he leaves without a degree. Apart from riding, golf, the ballet and his London club, his two chief concerns remain his poetry, which he is in the fortunate position of being able to publish (or impulsively destroy) at his own expense, and his emerging homosexuality. By the time war was declared, Sassoon had broken into literary circles with the help of his uncle's friend, Edmund Gosse, although he was soon to alienate the Grand Old Man with his poem 'Conscripts' (p69, *The War Poems*). Even more usefully, he had made contact with Edward Marsh, the moving force behind Georgianism and a respected critic. His advice to Sassoon to "write either with one's eye on an object or with one's mind at grips with a more or less definite idea" chimed with the young man's own feelings. But he could still only churn out Victorian pastiches.

The trenches transformed Sassoon and his poetry. Like many who joined up (although he was older than most) he had little concept of what he was to meet; but choosing at first to be a mere trooper rather than a commissioned officer, he might have guessed it would not be plain sailing. News of the death of Rupert Brooke perhaps brought reality closer, but in these early weeks he seemed more interested in the horses he helped care for and he had still not quite found his distinctive voice as a poet. It was only after he had recovered from a broken arm and become, like Robert Graves, an officer in the Royal Welch Fusiliers that something happened to his verse. It coincides with the start of a profound friendship with David Thomas, the death of his brother Hamo at Gallipoli and his arrival in November 1915 at Le Hamel on the front line. Here he wrote 'The Redeemer' (p16, *The War Poems*), with its audacious repeated assertion about the struggling soldier in a work-party ("I say that He was Christ"), culminating in what would become a characteristic highlighting of the ironies in colloquial usage: "O Christ Almighty, now I'm stuck!" With a bang, we have escaped the Victorians and the Sassoon 'biopic' zooms into close-up: he becomes Mad Jack, winner of the Military Cross, furious at God for destroying his beloved David; he becomes the friend (and premature elegist) of Graves; the mentor of Wilfred Owen at Craiglockhart; he becomes the author of the notorious *Statement* of July 1917, who cast more than the ribbon of his medal into the Mersey when he declared: "I believe that this War is being deliberately prolonged by those who have the power to end it ... I have seen and endured the sufferings of the troops, and I can no longer be a party to prolonging those sufferings for ends which I believe to be evil and unjust ..."

We leave what Auden called the "shilling life", and turn instead to Rupert Hart-Davis' 1983 chronological selection, *The War Poems*, which includes texts never published by Sassoon and also adds commentary by the poet together with textual background: where necessary, I have supplied a page reference to this edition, since the Sassoon estate imposes certain restrictions on longer quotations from the work. It is hard to imagine what an impact these poems must have had as they were published or sent off to influential friends: 'The Hero', 'The Road', 'They', 'Base Details', 'To Any Dead Officer', 'Does It Matter?'... It must have seemed as if someone had started lobbing Mills bombs from the trenches back to the London clubs. There is certainly shock, not to say panic, in some of the reactions that are on record. These little masterpieces are characterised by their coils of barbed rhyme, their deadly final couplets: "And no one seemed to care/Except that lonely woman with white hair."; "And when the war is done and youth stone dead,/ I'll toddle safely home and die – in bed."; "Cheero!/I wish they'd killed you in a decent show." That choice of rhyme-word, "show" brings out the element of play (again, one thinks of the "ever-popular war-game" in *Oh What a Lovely War!*) that Sassoon picks on, following from Newbolt's celebrated "Play up! Play up! and play the game!" Those on the Front soon saw that the Battle of the Somme, for example, was a huge board game being played by absent players with real lives. "He's a cheery old card!" is muttered under Harry's breath as the General passes. Yes, and both Harry and Jack are low denominations in his hand.

Very often in Sassoon's work there is earthy conversation (a knack learned from Hardy and Kipling, developed by several war poets, particularly Robert Nichols) and the interweaving of colloquialisms. This is not only the language of the soldiers but what Gurney called the "finicking accent" of home (see the last line of stanza 3 in 'Does It Matter?', p91, *The War Poems*) He reserves special gall for the delicate irrelevancies of women "back home", for whom this war was ostensibly being fought; and the sentiments of his 'Glory of Women' (p100) have been suitably rebuffed by Judith Kazantzis in her preface to the anthology of women's poetry, *Scars Upon My Heart*. Unsurprisingly, given his sexual preferences, Sassoon did not find it easy or take much trouble to get on with women: even Lady 'Utterly Immoral' Ottoline Morrell received short shrift when she tried to approach too close to him. But although it is true that Sassoon could be 'unfair' in a poem such as 'Their Frailty' (p101) he does catch the spirit of the age in lines 5-6 of 'Glory of Women'; and there is plenty of evidence in popular songs alone that women were encouraging men to go and fight. More to the point, the words of women were not the sole target of Sassoon's mockery: he attacked the remarks of ignorant politicians, self-important journalists, passing generals, and cheering "smug-faced crowds", not to mention the deserters and malingerers among his comrades. Frequently there is just a generalised fury directed at the whole country, as in 'Fight to a Finish' (p96), where there is acid in the phrase "refrained from dying".

Like so many of the war poets, but more dramatically than most, Sassoon is obliged to find room for new words, new rhythms, and something has to go. Craig Raine writes of Sassoon's "syntactical rickets" and his addiction to "literary artifice", but there is little of that in the best of his front-line poetry. He is handling words which are as strange to him as the weapons and tools they describe. We take for granted nowadays that a tank is a tank, forgetting that the name was only dreamt up to confuse the Germans about what they were going to be seeing. Sassoon was quick to pick up metaphorical uses of war language, too: "you're beyond the wire", for example, meaning "you are dead" in 'To Any Dead Officer' (p82); and in the third stanza of the same poem we find him exploiting the cruel paradoxes that troopers were only too aware of and which became a favourite topic: how a desperate desire to live is often a death sentence. And the chatty final stanza can only have been written in a world where telegraph, telephone and wireless had suddenly become strategically vital. Of course, in 1917, when this was written, the possibility of communicating with the dead was very much in people's minds, too, but Sassoon is not really interested in spiritualism and we are an age beyond Browning's very uncolloquial Mr Sludge.

Nowhere do we see more clearly the distance Siegfried Sassoon has come from the Tintern Abbey School of verse than when he writes of ruins – no longer picturesque and Gothic, but ruins such as those described in 'Prelude: The Troops' (p104). Sassoon's best poems are about the ghastly inappropriateness of the resources of poetic language that any poet of 1914 would naturally bring with him. David Jones and others on the Home Front were going to find other ways of expressing the fragmentation of a culture, but Sassoon clung at least to the old metres and stanza-forms, if not quite agreeing with what Hardy told Robert Graves, that "all we can do is write about the old themes in the old styles". He would never be at his best trying to evoke breakdown: that he must leave to Owen, and more to Eliot. 'Repression of War Experience', one of his blank verse pieces, attempts to go deeper, but he can only write 'about' the experience, using repetition and italics for emphasis, not carrying us into the depths of his feelings with the rhythm or the imagery. Yet in his short, rhymed poems he was discovering depths of a different kind: perfecting a way of tunnelling under the jauntiness of ballad and conventional metre, of blowing up cant and hypocrisy with irony.

He often wrote best when he wasn't really trying, when he was away from the physical proximity of the trenches, when he allowed his unconscious mind to lead him. 'They' (p57) was written in October 1916 in (appropriately) Half Moon Street at 1 a.m. when (he writes) "I was so sleepy I could hardly keep my eyes open, but the thing just wrote itself." 'They' is typical in its structure: two stanzas confronting each other across the No Man's Land where everything is transformed. In the first stanza, the Bishop preaches on the wondrous transformation that war will have wrought in the boys when they come back. Sassoon simply gives us the Bishop's words, knowing that they provide the best foil for the truth (*Vero nihil verius*), that their absurdity provides all the ammunition he needs to win this particular campaign. Of course the boys "will not be the same", and it seems inconceivable now that anyone should speak of anything other than shellshock and war wounds, but the surprise comes with the deft enjambments: "In a just cause", then "On Anti-Christ". The withered 'Ancient and Modern' phraseology – "bought", "breed" – the personification of Death in an avoidance of confronting it "face to face"...

Then, the other side of this coin, etched in clear monosyllables ("syphilitic" and "Bishop" two of the exceptions) that mock the "honourable" and "Anti-Christ" we have just heard, Sassoon offers the soldiers' reply. He has them intone, like an intercessional prayer, a list of the wounds suffered by George, Bill, Jim and Bert, to which the Bishop can only mutter something about God's ways being strange.

This satirical note does not really come to the fore in English culture again until the satirical television shows of the 1960s. Sassoon adds an amusing footnote to 'They' in *The War Poems*: as he walked back from showing the poem to Edward Marsh at 10 Downing Street, wondering what Marsh had meant when he called it "*too* horrible", Sassoon recalls, "I actually met 'The Bishop' (of London) and he turned a mild shining gaze on me and my MC."

Despite his mockery of the Church, Sassoon was an instinctively religious soul and there is an element of prayer in many of his poems, although less during the bloodiest episodes of the war. 'Before the Battle' (p39), however, from June 1916, makes an invocation of its Yeatsian refrain. This seems to be an appeal to the local nature gods: they give him comfort so that he has "no need to pray/That fear may pass away". There is a sly wink to his struggling faith in a rather more convincing, slightly later poem, 'The One-Legged Man'(p48), in which a soldier, able at last to enjoy at least some of the basic human rights, thanks God that his leg had to be amputated.

All the norms of civilised life are turned upside down – so Sassoon even inverts a sonnet ('The Tombstone-Maker') to suggest as much.

In this poem, the craftsman ruefully remarks on the scores of corpses that haven't been given a decent burial. While in 'Stretcher Case' the casualty revels in the sight of banal advertising hoardings which under different circumstances would be an irritating vulgarity: "Lung Tonic, Mustard, Liver Pills and Beer". Here at least it is not mustard gas and his lungs are safe. Sassoon depicts this surreal world without ever becoming a surrealist himself. A journalist he has been called – but a good poet needs to be part journalist, particularly when he feels a responsibility to report the truth to those who do not know it. A poem like 'Attack' (p95) shows him simply and effectively saying "what happened" as he recollects events from the enforced haven of Craiglockhart in 1917. Except for the final outburst ("O Jesus, make it stop!") and the rather lavish description of the sunrise, these 13 lines of present tense could almost be an outside broadcast by a veteran commentator. Imagine it in the voice of David (or Richard) Dimbleby: "At dawn the ridge emerges ..."

Naturally, Siegfried Sassoon's passionate anti-war stance meant that his poems frequently have what Keats did not like poems to have – a "palpable design" on us. But while he might not be able to answer Keats, Sassoon would have a fitting riposte to Auden who claimed in his elegy on Yeats that "poetry makes nothing happen". It is probable that the writings of Sassoon influenced many people; he had the ear of those in power. As Minister of Munitions, Churchill seldom went anywhere without a copy of Sassoon's *Counter-Attack*, and apparently knew much of it by heart. Sassoon's biographer, John Stuart Roberts, relates that Lord Esher was so curious about Churchill's public renderings of these poems that he wrote to the poet's cousin, who was on General Haig's staff, asking "Who is Siegfried Sassoon?".

'Aftermath'(p143) is from the next collection Sassoon published, following *Counter-Attack*, so Churchill might not have known it; but it is a good example of the kind of poem that could make something happen. It could worm into people's memories as those other poems did into Churchill's, and it could set them thinking. At the very least it could make people remember: "*Look down, and swear by the slain of the War that you'll never forget.*"

Further Reading

Collected Poems (Faber, 1984)
Memoirs of an Infantry Officer (Faber, 1930)
The War Poems (ed. Hart-Davis, Faber, 1983)

* * *

Moorcroft Wilson, Jean, *Siegfried Sassoon: the Journey from the Trenches* (Duckworth, 2003)

Raine, Craig, essay in *Haydn and the Valve-Trumpet* (Faber, 1990)

Roberts, John Stuart, *Siegfried Sassoon* (Richard Cohen Books, 1999)

Silkin, Jon, *Out of Battle* (Routledge and Kegan Paul, 1972)

8

Wilfrid Gibson 1878-1962

All the poets discussed so far had experience of the Front and it might be assumed from the more frequently anthologised poems by Wilfrid Gibson that he too had spent time in France. Indeed, the few books that do discuss him at any length (and many key volumes don't bother) take him at his word when he describes the cruel ironies of battle in the first person, as he does in the popular 'Breakfast' from 1916. But in a recent collection of brief lives, Tonie and Valmai Holt suggest that Gibson "never went anywhere near a trench; his war poetry is a great feat of imaginative writing based on solid research." How far this is true it is difficult to establish, as facts about this poet's life during the war are as scarce as volumes of his once best-selling poetry. Gibson deliberately covered his tracks, believing – like at least one rather better-known contemporary – that the biography should not be allowed to obscure the work.

This certainly raises questions about how far our appreciation of war poets depends on knowing that they saw action. It is like the special piquancy that comes with knowing that a film is 'based on a true story'. But then if the truth turns out to have been stretched … Something similar happened with Robert Graves' *Goodbye To All That*, which the author later claimed to have been much elaborated and exaggerated with an eye to what "the age demanded". Yet as it stood, Graves' work had a good few of his contemporaries (notably Sassoon) running in panic for their blue pencils. And I do not think that there were many complaints about the inaccuracy of Gibson's accounts of battle. The twinge of guilt in one of his finest poems, 'Lament', suggests that perhaps the Holts' theory is correct:

We who are left, how shall we look again
Happily on the sun or feel the rain,
Without remembering how they who went
Ungrudgingly, and spent
Their all for us, loved too the sun and rain?

A bird among the rain-wet lilac sings—
But we, how shall we turn to little things
And listen to the birds and winds and streams
Made holy by their dreams,
Nor feel the heart-break in the heart of things?

This is the final poem in a short cycle, 'Casualties', published two
years after the war. Its tone echoes Binyon's much earlier 'For the
Fallen' and the pair of questions reminds us of the similar structure
of 'Anthem for Doomed Youth'. Owen at least provided answers.
'Lament' demonstrates Gibson's sensitivity to syntax, crucial in a
poet whose diction is perilously plain. Rhyme tends to intrude in
some of his earlier pastoral poems, but here it is moving in its aptness.
The last line's weight and pace are beautifully judged. It is important
to keep such achievements in mind while reading Gibson, since he
produced so much and was not always very self-critical. Nevertheless,
this particular cycle, 'Casualties', is worth exploring and deserves
to be more widely known. The fourteen short poems are snapshots
of individuals on the Front, showing the circumstances of their deaths.
Few are longer than eight lines, but they convey as well as anything
of the period the relentlessness and utter humourlessness of the ironies
at work. 'Peter Proudfoot' consists of three lines:

He cleaned out middens for his daily bread:
War took him overseas and in a bed
Of lilies-of-the-valley dropt him dead.

The story of 'Joe Barnes' is slightly longer:

To a proud peacock strutting tail-in-air
He clipped the yew each thirteenth of July—
No feather ruffled, sleek and debonair,
Clean-edged it cut the yellow evening sky.

But he returns no more, who went across
The narrow seas one thirteenth of July;
And drearily all day the branches toss,
Ragged and dark against the rainy sky.

Such pieces give the lie to Larkin's remark in a letter of 1968: "Gibson, for instance – a lifetime of books, ending with a Macmillan's *Collected Poems* just like Yeats or Hardy or C. Rossetti. *Never wrote a good poem in his life.*" In fact, Larkin gives himself the lie elsewhere, as when he calls Gibson a "much underestimated poet" and includes six and a half pages of his work in his Oxford anthology. Other than in such collections (together with a small press reprint of *Battle* and an unsatisfactory edition to celebrate the 125th anniversary of his birth) there has not been a representative selection of Gibson's work published since Charles Williams edited one for Faber at the end of the Second World War (*Solway Ford and Other Poems*), but this only gives the barest idea of his achievement as a war poet.

Wilfrid Wilson Gibson came from Hexham, where he was born in the appropriately named Battle Hill Terrace. His father was himself something of a writer as well as an amateur archaeologist and photographer, but he earned his living as a chemist. The Gibsons' shop was so typical of its time that a replica was made for the Science Museum, where it can apparently still be seen. Wilfrid's health was never good and he had poor eyesight. Perhaps because of this he was largely educated by a sister. But he was clearly something of a prodigy and had a poem in the *Spectator* before he was 20. Collections of verse followed: *The Golden Helm* (1902) and *Stonefolds* (1907). In this latter volume and even more in *Daily Bread* (1910) he began to write less about myth and more about his own back yard, the local mining people of Northumberland. Gibson always responded to what was near and immediate. Robert Frost, who had initially warmed to him as a man of the people, came to see this as a revealing limitation, citing the occasion when they had together visited a point-to-point meeting and Wilfrid said to him, "I didn't see a thing there I could use, did you?" Their friendship turned very sour and an incident in 1915 where Gibson failed to support his friend in a confrontation with a gamekeeper did not help matters. Frost called him "the worst snob I met in England ... a coward and a snob" and took some potshots in later reviews of *Solway Ford.*

Daily Bread had been through three editions by 1913 and Gibson was having success with magazines in America, when he decided that he needed to go to London. Portraits of him at this time show a rather severe profile, glasses pinched to his nose, the obligatory loose cravat, a touch of self-consciousness, with something pettish around the lips. He looks as though he wants to be up and gone. He found lodgings with the help of Kathleen Mansfield and Middleton Murry (who liked the poet's "singular integrity") and was soon rubbing shoulders with literati. He had arrived at a good time, for Harold Monro had just opened his Poetry Bookshop and Edward Marsh's 'Georgian' anthologies were about to be launched. Apart from the obvious career advantages, he was also to find a bedsit above the bookshop and marry the shop assistant. The ubiquitous Marsh arranged anonymously for this budding poet from the north-east to work on his short-lived magazine, *Rhythm*, to free him from the burden of book-reviewing that was driving Edward Thomas, down in Gloucestershire, to the verge of despair. Gibson soon made plans for a publishing venture of his own (*New Numbers*) and was to head for Thomas' part of the world, but not before he had met the most important friend he was ever to make: Rupert Brooke, whose personality and charisma haunted his verse for the rest of his life. Brooke was so fond of Gibson (or "Wibson" as he called him) that he left him a legacy: a share in the proceeds of his monumentally successful *Poetical Works*.

The Old Nail Shop is one of the places that anyone in search of that fascinating period-piece of a 'movement', the Dymock Poets, will visit. Earlier chapters have dealt with something of this period, when Frost and Thomas made those famous walks together, but all the while Wilfrid Gibson and his new Irish wife were ensconced nearby 'under thatch' (much to Frost's envy – his "best friend" Wilfrid had not managed to find the same for him at Little Iddens). The newly-weds were deliriously happy together – so much so that Marsh wrote that Gibson's Muse "seems to have yielded her place to Miss T". Very often Frost and Thomas would be turned away by Geraldine because her husband was working. He, after all, was the success of the group (*Fires* came out in 1912, *Thoroughfares* and *Borderlands* both in 1914) and Frost complained that Gibson, once anything but a "literary poseur" now tended to regard himself as England's greatest poet. They were still there when war broke out and Gibson's 1925 poem 'The Golden Room', with its heady nostalgia, marks a gathering of Brooke, Frost, Thomas and the Abercrombies which most likely took place on 24th June 1914, just four days before Archduke Ferdinand's assassination:

> Now, on the crest of an Aegean isle,
> Brooke sleeps, and dreams of England: Thomas lies
> 'Neath Vimy Ridge, where he, among his fellows,
> Died, just as life had touched his lips to song ...

Gibson's chief claim to fame in the early war years is the publishing of Brooke's famous sonnets (touchingly echoed above) in the first *New Numbers*. It was probably he who changed the title of "If I should die ..." from 'The Recruit' to 'The Soldier'. Brooke's death marked the end of the Dymock Poets and indeed of the Georgians. But it was the beginning of the War Poetry. For Gibson, Brooke's end was his beginning, financially speaking. For the rest of his life he was comfortably off. He died 12 years after his wife in a nursing home in Virginia Water on 26th May 1962. And he left £10,000 – quite a sum for a poet. He had published another 12 volumes of poetry between 1920 and 1950, but after the Thirties Poets, the Apocalyptics, the Movement, not to mention Alvarez's *New Poetry* — nobody was very interested in W.W. Gibson.

What, though, of that service record? Having always suffered from poor health – dietary problems, an appendix removed in 1916 – and abysmal eyesight, he was rejected by the Army four times. In between applications, he found time for a reading tour of the USA (December 1916 – July 1917) until eventually – and it is rumoured that Edward Marsh had a hand in this – he was accepted. Here the record grows hazy, except that whatever he did, he seems to have hated it. According to the Holts, he was a driver with the Army Service Corps in London and then a clerk to a medical officer. Other sources speak of him spending "a few months at the Front", but loading lorries and, wherever he was, his poem 'The Chart' suggests the tedium of his work, a far cry from the scenes of battle he had so vividly evoked. Another rumour has it that he was so unhappy that he tried to have Marsh arrange his discharge. Whatever the truth in this, he was not out until 1919, when he resumed his round of lectures and readings.

Most of Gibson's war poems are included in that Macmillan *Collected* edition mentioned by Larkin, although its mere eight hundred pages only cover the period from 1905 – 1925 and there are other sequences in later volumes, notably 'Aftermath' in *Hazards* (1928-30). The section from the *Collected Poems* titled 'Battle' (1916) gives a fair idea of Gibson's quick-fire ability, although some of the more finely crafted poems turn up in later pages: sonnets, in particular, such as '1916', 'Troopship: Mid-Atlantic' or 'The Conscript'. 'Battle' has the immediacy and roughness of an artist's sketchbook. Almost all the poems are short, using repetition and rhyme in an obsessive, hallucinatory way, sometimes like a folk-song or a ballad and often depending for their effect on a sudden surprise or irony:

> ... All day in the wurzels 'neath the Belgian sun:
> But among this little lot
> It's a different job I've got—
> For you don't hoe mangel-wurzels with a gun.

'Mangel-Wurzels' is not Gibson at his best but it shows much that is typical. The simplicity, the faux-naivety of this style is about as far as can be imagined from Blunden's dense Arcadian thickets or indeed from the kind of visions Edward Thomas conjured from beet and turnip. Gibson does not engage with the natural world as those poets do; rather, as Robert Frost noted, he 'uses' it. His poem about a lark singing at the Front (in which the rhyming dictionary has evidently been raided for the word 'brattle') has nothing like the authenticity of Thomas' or even Sassoon's birdsong poems – not to mention Ralph Vaughan Williams' lark ascending at much the same moment from the trenches. Wilfrid Gibson the War Poet, like Wilfrid Gibson the Nature Poet, has a fairly limited range of tricks. He likes the jolt, the "simple antithesis" remarked upon by Paul Fussell in *The Great War and Modern Memory,* whereby men are at one minute pursuing some trivial task and the next they are gone. So many times and so unaffectedly does Gibson write about this, that one comes from his books with a powerful sense of the loss of *individuals* – something that the grander orchestrations of his contemporaries do not always achieve. No one poem in 'Battle' could be called really successful, but Gibson's productivity was such that he could fashion a mosaic recording the experience of the trenches in an unsentimental, matter-of-fact way that may seem dated in 2004, but which few other writers of the period manage. Plenty, of course, have managed it in the intervening years. 'The Joke' is just one of his tesserae:

> He'd even have his joke
> While we were sitting tight,
> And so he needs must poke
> His silly head in sight
> To whisper some new jest,
> Chortling, but as he spoke
> A rifle cracked ...
> And now God knows when I shall hear the rest.

This 'jolt' is a device which Gibson uses in other 'non-combat' poems such as that old school anthology favourite, 'The Ice-Cart', but it is obviously particularly suited to the subject of war. His rhymes, which can be irritatingly unsubtle, add here to the impact of sudden death – as they do for example, in 'Hit'. Gibson is less interested in using rhyme's sharp edge for anger or mockery. One of his later sonnets, 'Ragtime', nevertheless, covers the same territory as Sassoon's well-known 'Blighters', where an appalled rift is torn between the two quatrains, the whole poem driven by fury. In Gibson's sonnet, octave confronts sestet, and the poet's eventual response is more restrained, thoughtful, leading to another of his sensitively balanced concluding cadences, although there is just as much alliterative fury accumulated in the syntax and diction of the opening:

> A Minx in khaki struts the limelit boards:
> With false moustache, set smirk, and ogling eyes
> And straddling legs and swinging hips she tries
> To swagger it like a soldier ...

As Fussell says: " ... antithesis ... is the atmosphere in which most of the poems of the Great War take place and that is the reason for the failure of most of them as durable art." For Gibson, it was enough to let the juxtapositions speak for themselves, as in 'The Glorious Dead', which is hardly a 'Dulce Et Decorum Est ', but it makes its point:

> He talked about 'the glorious dead,'
> And how we always should remember them;
> And then she turned on him and said—
> *If you mean Willie, Dick and Jem,*
> *The living lads they took from me*
> *To blow to pieces with artillery—*
> *Much good to them 'twill do*
> *To be remembered by the likes of you ...*

Gibson is on familiar territory here, but he does also explore unexpected thematic areas and the little-known poems in his 1930 collection *Hazards* (from which 'The Glorious Dead' comes) are a good example. Particularly moving is the sequence on 'The Silence' in which we hear what ordinary people think during the two minutes on Armistice Day: "Two minutes' silence! Nay, but there has been/ For fourteen years a silence in my heart ..." Other poems pick up on a theme Gibson circled round in 'Battle' and touched on in the loose Sapphics of its splendid final poem, the idea of the soldier who has died but does not realise he is dead:

> I could not understand the sudden quiet—
> The sudden darkness, in the crash of fight,
> The din and glare of day quenched in a twinkling
> In utter starless night.

It should not be forgotten that one of the most popular books during this war was Sir Oliver Lodge's *Raymond*, which tells of this eminent physicist's attempts at communicating with the spirit of his son who had died at the Front. Gibson must have been aware of this work; the style of his own writing, however, suggests that he had been spending more time reading his old rival Robert Frost, to whom *Hazards* is dedicated. Frost certainly knew the haunting power of suppressed trauma as 'Home Burial' alone will testify. Gibson's 'Aftermath' poems never quite achieve anything on that scale, but they are full of the nervy after-effects of war ('The Luck' or 'The Broken Latch'), the madness, the disbelief, the sudden horrified realisation and, in 'Meeting in Wartime', downright spookiness – reminding us that Gibson's most anthologised poem of all is 'Flannan Isle', about the disappearing lighthouse keepers:

He passed me by, as one who walks in dream,
Without a smile or word, to my surprise:
And then I knew the meaning of the gleam
In those strange still unrecognising eyes.

Further Reading

Collected Poems 1905-1925 (Macmillan, 1933)
Battle (ed. R.K.R. Thornton, Cyder Press, University of Gloucester)
Hazards, Poems 1928-1930 (Macmillan, 1930)
Homecoming (Wagtail Press, Hexham, 2003)
Solway Ford and other poems (ed. Charles Williams, Faber, 1945)

* * *

Clark, Keith, *The Muse Colony* (Redcliffe, 1992)
Fussell, Paul, *The Great War and Modern Memory* (OUP, 1975)
Holt, Tonie & Valmai, *Violets from Oversea* (Leo Cooper, London, 1996)
Street, Sean, *The Dymock Poets* (Seren Books, 1994)

9

Charles Sorley 1895-1915
Robert Graves 1895-1985

Robert Graves was the oldest of the war poets when he died; Charles Sorley was the youngest. Since there are several other parallels between the two, not least their sympathy for the German nation, it seems fitting to discuss them side by side. Graves was very excited to discover Sorley's poetry and wrote to Edward Marsh enthusiastically. His poem 'Sorley's Weather' is "a gentle song" made in memory of his peer. In it, the poet is enjoying the peace, comfort and warmth of his study while "the winds blow strong", and though tempted to escape from what those winds might bring by drinking deep of the Romantic Poets, he concludes, with an outrageous rhyme and a very Gravesian touch of the supernatural:

> Yet rest there, Shelley, on the sill,
> > For though the winds come frorely
> I'm away to the rain-blown hill
> > And the ghost of Sorley.

Charles Hamilton Sorley was born (with his twin brother) in Aberdeen on 19th May 1895, two months before Graves. His father became a Professor of Moral Philosophy at Cambridge five years later and so the poet's wanderings began: in fact, 'Sorley' means 'wanderer', as the Gaelic poet of the Second World War Sorley MacLean would have known. From King's College Choir School he won a scholarship to Marlborough, where he proved athletic, extremely intelligent, a keen debater with socialist leanings. Here too, he discovered his love of nature in which (as Ian Parsons writes): "he saw, though dimly, an interpretation of the meaning and purpose of existence". He always felt close to his old school, corresponding with its headmaster, and recalling its downland surroundings with its Schubertian footpath signs in poems such as 'Lost' and the first of his 'Two Sonnets' (1915). His only collection is titled *Marlborough and Other Poems*. This ran into six editions in the year of its publication, 1916.

In January 1914 Sorley wandered to Germany to prepare himself for a course in philosophy and economics at the University of Jena. He is one of the few First World War poets to actually show an understanding and even a love of German culture, to express admiration for their work ethic and their precision thinking. He is only being half-playful when he says, "I felt that perhaps I could die for *Deutschland* – and I have never had an inkling of that feeling about England and never shall." Yet he was quick to condemn the anti-Semitism at Jena, and suggests once the war has begun that they are "not fighting a bully, but a bigot". Naturally, once conflict became inevitable he had to leave Germany, which he did by the skin of his teeth, having been arrested and thrown into prison on the day before England declared war.

One can imagine how difficult it was for Sorley to find himself back in England in August 1914 ("England – I am sick of the sound of the word") yet he did not hesitate to apply for a commission, flagellating himself the while:

> What a worm one is under the cart-wheels – big clumsy careless lumbering cart-wheels – of public opinion. I might have been giving my mind to fight against Sloth and Stupidity; instead, I am giving my body (by a refinement of cowardice) to fight against the most enterprising nation in the world.

His sonnet 'To Germany' is unique among war poems: "You are blind like us ..." it begins, and although history teaches us that Germany was, if anything, 'blind' to its own atrocities in the early days of the war, Sorley convinces us for 14 lines that humanity's common quest is what matters : "But gropers both through fields of thought confined/We stumble and we do not understand ..."

But it was to France that the rest of his life would be dedicated. Joining the Suffolk Regiment in September, he was billeted in Nieppe by the end of May 1915. Yet his passion for poetry grew ever stronger, unafraid to criticise "arid" Hardy for his 'Men Who March Away', to express delight that Kipling "hasn't written a poem yet" and especially harsh on Rupert Brooke, who seemed to him "too obsessed with his own sacrifice". His discomfort at these self-appointed poetic spokesmen of the war is clear in 'To Poets', which (albeit somewhat clumsily) lets the soldier tell the poet what he thinks of him, that "We too make music" although "We have no comeliness like you". He even awarded himself an imaginary prize for 'Whom Therefore We Ignorantly Worship', because he considered it to be the first unpatriotic poem since 4th August.

Sorley had a fairly shrewd idea of how the war was going, as his letters show: "War in England only means putting all the men of 'military age' in England into a state of routinal coma, preparatory to getting them killed ... We don't seem to be winning, do we? It looks like an affair of years", adding the usual prayer for a 'Blighty One': "a nice little bullet wound (tidy and clean) in the shoulder". These fine letters, together with the handful of poems he deposited with his family before he embarked for France in May 1915, are all we have to read by C.H. Sorley. His parents were keen to publish his poems when they saw them, but he restrained them as "I have had no time for the final touch". Among them were these celebrated, untitled, lines:

> All the hills and vales along
> Earth is bursting into song,
> And the singers are the chaps
> Who are going to die perhaps ...

Written before he had experienced the trenches, nevertheless the consciously over-enthusiastic opening and the ironic insouciance of "perhaps" strikes a note that would not be out of place in *Oh What a Lovely War!* Sorley's tone in his letters and poems can sometimes sound like the exhilaration we find in Grenfell's 'Into Battle', when more often he is (as Jon Silkin explains) "jocular, even wryly self-conscious". One should not read this poem as one might Sassoon's, with dark double-meanings in every line, but Sorley was too intelligent a man not to know what he was implying when he wrote: "So be glad, when you are sleeping" or "So sing with joyful breath,/ For why, you are going to death." He did regard himself as having "ultra-strong religious instincts", but surely this cannot be read as a Revivalist marching hymn. If anything, the third stanza echoes the drily amused tone of young Chidiock Tichborne waiting to be executed ("And now I live, and now my life is done"):

> Pour your gladness on earth's head,
> So be merry, so be dead.

Yet 'All the Hills and Vales Along' does rise to something more triumphant by the end, suggesting not only Sorley's strong Wiltshire-bred instinct for the enduring power of nature, but also his divided loyalties when it came to fighting Germany:

> All the music of their going,
> Ringing swinging glad song-throwing,
> Earth will echo still, when foot
> Lies numb and voice mute.

Billeted in Nieppe, Sorley composed there his 'Two Sonnets', whose opposition of the idealised and the down-to-earth must have appealed to Graves, fascinated as he was by such polarities: we know that he particularly liked the second, which begins with admirable clarity and directness:

> Such, such is Death: no triumph: no defeat:
> Only an empty pail, a slate rubbed clean,
> A merciful putting away of what has been.

He saw action around the notorious Ypres Salient and led a bombing raid on 'Brother Boche' (as he had learnt to call the Germans), who were less than 70 yards away in his particular sector. One of his men was wounded by his own grenade and Sorley had to drag him back. He became second in command of his company and experienced a typically badly organised push in Loos at the end of September. He died on 13th October, hit by machine-gun fire, and his body was never recovered. In his kitbag was his rather Owen-like untitled sonnet, beginning "When you see millions of the mouthless dead/ Across your dreams in pale battalions go,/Say not soft things as other men have said,/That you'll remember. For you need not so." The ghostly procession would, again, have attracted Graves, who felt himself a haunted man, personally saw the "spook" of one Private Challoner killed at Festubert, and wrote in *Goodbye to All That* of the "numerous ghosts in France". Jon Silkin suggests that the line "Say only this, 'They are dead'" could be read as a comment on Brooke's "If I should die, think only this of me ..."

When Sorley died, Graves was struck by the similarities between them. Writing to Edward Marsh he expressed what hopes he had had for this loveable young poet. Born in the same year, at public school during the same period, sent to France in the same month, sharing a similar breezy insouciance about the war, but also a rare appreciation of what Germany meant, producing a similar amount of poetry about the war, the difference between Graves and Sorley was that whereas the latter was dead at 20, the former would go on to live into the fifth year of Mrs Thatcher's government. As Sorley put it: "This died, that went his way".

Robert Graves was fascinated by such "simple antithesis", which Paul Fussell identifies as the key to "the atmosphere in which most of the poems of the Great War take place". The title of Graves' best-known war-time collection, *Fairies and Fusiliers* is just one of many such couplings (Gurney's *Severn and Somme* is another) and many of his poems depend on juxtapositions, coincidences, contrasts thrown up by fate:

> Near Martinpuisch that night of hell
> Two men were struck by the same shell,
> Together tumbling in one heap
> Senseless and limp like slaughtered sheep.
> 'The Leveller'

Graves was always on the look-out for a doppelgänger, that 'Other Man' that Edward Thomas never quite caught up with. If he knew that Sorley was himself a twin, it would surely have interested Graves the myth-maker, the future author of *The White Goddess* who would argue that there was always a rival for the attentions of the muse. He was himself a divided man, half German, half Irish, personified I think in the speakers of his poem 'Welsh Incident', one of whom wants the facts, and the other simply enjoys embroidering: "I was coming to that ..." It was perhaps the Celtic side of his parentage that drew him to Yeatsian mysteries and made him feel more than usually haunted after the war. He certainly writes more ghost poems than anyone except perhaps Gibson. 'Haunted' and 'Corporal Stare' (about Private Challoner), the Hardyesque 'An Occasion', 'The Survivor' and even 'Tom Taylor' spring to mind among those with war as the theme. Naturally, in a character of such antitheses, Graves is also a shrewd pragmatist, and could conjure a 'Sergeant-Major Money' as well as a 'Corporal Stare'. *Goodbye to All That* was written strictly for money and not only did it enable him to abscond to Majorca with Laura Riding, but it helped alienate his good friends Siegfried Sassoon and Edmund Blunden since he played fast and loose with the facts of the war in order to make it entertaining.

Robert Graves' German background caused him a good deal of difficulty at Charterhouse, where 'German' meant 'dirty German' to the boys, and to have 'von Ranke' as your middle name would not have impressed the Royal Welch Fusiliers either, whom he joined when war broke out. But it did help him to communicate with the piteous detainees at an internment camp he was sent to on detachment duty, assuring the various travelling salesmen, sailors and family men caught up in the war, that they were "safer inside than out". And it enabled him to produce poems with a surprising perspective, such as 'The Savage Story of Cardonette', about a massacre of German soldiers, and even adds a knowing piquancy to his 'Armistice Day, 1918':

> Now they'll hang Kaiser Bill from a lamp-post,
> Von Tirpitz they'll hang from a tree...
> We've been promised a 'Land Fit for Heroes'—
> What heroes we heroes must be!

Although Graves spent time with relatives in Germany and followed their colourful war careers with interest, he was more affected by the Welsh landscape, which he harks back to in 'Big Words' and 'Over the Brazier'.

Before leaving for France in May 1915, he wrote 'It's a Queer Time', in which he anticipates trench life without having actually experienced it, the peculiarly Gravesian note being his attempt to blur childhood experience with the horror of battle:

It's hard to know if you're alive or dead
When steel and fire go roaring through your head.

One moment you'll be crouching at your gun
Traversing, mowing heaps down half in fun:
The next, you choke and clutch at your right breast –
No time to think – leave all – and off you go …
To Treasure Island where the Spice winds blow …

He was obviously rather proud of the accuracy of his jaunty but by
no means ineffective account, although he criticised Robert Nichols
for doing much the same thing. Genuine trench experience was not
far away, however. He was firstly at Bethune, then near Loos and on
to Laventie (immortalised by Gurney), where the RWF officers
behaved like "damned snobs", disdaining to acknowledge that there
was a war on and preferring their polo matches. It was during this
August that Graves composed his sequence 'Nursery Memories'
which takes the idea used in 'It's a Queer Time' even further and
tells battlefield stories through the protective mask of childhood, a
German corpse becoming a dead dog buried by children, a machine-
gun attack turned into an imaginary tiger hunt, and a moonlight patrol
stirring childhood anxiety. There is something of Goethe's 'Erl King'
here:

I like the stars, and especially the Big Bear
  And the W star, and one like a diamond ring,
But I *hate* the Moon and its horrible stony stare,
  And I know one day it'll do me some dreadful thing.

The child's-eye view of the world intrigued Graves, but in 'The Next
War', he feels obliged to warn the younger generation not to be taken
in by the Newbolts of the world: "Happy though these hours you
spend,/Have they warned you how games end?"

   In another parallel with Sorley, Graves was unhappy with much
of his war poetry and excluded it from his various *Collected* editions.
It was not generally available until William Graves published his
father's *Poems About War*, which included everything that could be
found on the subject. There are several fine poems, mostly from
1915, which supplement Graves' vivid prose descriptions in *Goodbye*

to *All That*: 'The Morning Before the Battle', 'Limbo', 'Trench Life'. 'Retrospect: the Jests of the Clock' dates from just after the war and takes a broader view, considering the soldier "chained to the sodden ground,/Rotting alive" and a martyr to "the jests of the clock". Graves said in a television interview that he swore after the war that he would never again work for any boss: he clearly hated fitting in with someone else's routine, preferring to work in his own "field or kailyard" and to share the "honest idiocy of flight" of the cabbage white butterfly. In this poem the exasperated narrator has "met hours of the clock he never guessed before":

> When noisome smells of day were sicklied by cold night,
> When sentries froze and muttered; when beyond the wire
> Blank shadows crawled and tumbled, shaking, tricking the sight,
> When impotent hatred of Life stifled desire ...

The circumstances are captured with unneurotic, playful Gravesian rhythms and euphonies ("shaking/tricking" "Life/stifled") sharply, colloquially, yet there is a real thrill of anxiety at those ghosts out in the dark of No Man's Land.

Despite the cheery note struck in so much of Graves' poetry, he suffered from 'progressive neurasthenia', heightened by news about a sex scandal involving an old friend of his from school. But a new friend awaited him at Locon: Siegfried Sassoon. The two men grew very fond of each other, Graves (not without considerable controversy) describing Sassoon in *Goodbye to All That* (1929) and Sassoon reciprocating by portraying Graves as David Cromlech in *Memoirs of an Infantry Officer* (1930). Sassoon had his doubts about Graves' war poetry, but then so did their author, and these are two reasons why they are not better known.

One event that affected both men profoundly was the death in March 1916 of their fellow officer David Thomas, who was shot while Graves was with him on a working party. The poem 'Goliath and David' is a parable in rhyming couplets which works in the same way as Wilfred Owen's of Abraham and Isaac. In the latter piece, Abraham decides to ignore the angel and kill his son "and all the seed of Europe one by one". In Graves', too, the Biblical authority is flouted and Goliath kills (Lieut.) David (Thomas): "God's eyes are dim. His ears are shut." Another, shorter poem, 'Not Dead' marks the event more poignantly and peacefully, although Graves tells us elsewhere that his instinct was to go out "looking for Germans to kill".

Graves went on leave in April, spending some time in London where he met Lloyd George, and only returned when there was a sudden demand for more men to replace those slaughtered on the first day of the Somme. He was back in Line by 5th July, relieved to find Sassoon still in one piece, but swiftly involved in the grim fighting at Mametz Wood about which he wrote the 'Familiar Letter to Siegfried Sassoon'. 'A Dead Boche' comes from this time too, the incident concerned being described in *Goodbye To All That*, but the economy and clear-eyed directness of these two six-line stanzas never fail to move. There's a touch of Hilaire Belloc's 'Cautionary Tales' in the opening:

> To you who'd read my songs of War
>   And only hear of blood and fame,
> I'll say (you've heard it said before)
>   'War's Hell!' …

And British understatement has never been so devastating as in:

> … and if you doubt the same,
> To-day I found in Mametz Wood
> A certain cure for lust of blood:

This friendly offering of some harmless quackery proves, of course, anything but understated, except in its quiet factual note and its refusal to rise to any brazen finale:

> Where, propped against a shattered trunk,
>   In a great mess of things unclean,
> Sat a dead Boche; he scowled and stunk
>   With clothes and face a sodden green,
> Big-bellied, spectacled, crop-haired,
> Dribbling black blood from nose and beard.

Graves, part-German himself, looks at what is now only part of a German in a ghastly shadow version of the way he will look in the mirror and write his self-portrait. Here again is the twin, the "blood-brother, the other self" (of which Graves spoke in one of several television interviews). The most bizarre manifestation of this was when Graves found himself reading his own obituary in *The Times*. On 20th July he was wounded by a shell and reported dead. His parents duly received notice of his death. The whole incident was wonderful material for a writer: he reminisces about it in 'Bazentin 1916', 'Escape' and 'Died of Wounds'.

Sorley had been truly dead for over a year when Graves was eventually passed unfit for further active service, his lungs having been so badly damaged at High Wood. He involved himself closely in Sassoon's protest and (according to Sassoon's biographer John Stuart Roberts) became "a key player" in discouraging his friend from publishing it, knowing he would be "court-martialled, cashiered and imprisoned". Sassoon, of course, wanted the publicity and Graves had to lie to him that he had been told "on the highest authority, that the military would never give him a court-martial" before he would agree to back down. Graves then went before the Medical Board on Sassoon's behalf, "a courageous act of friendship and loyalty" writes John Stuart Roberts, "from someone who was himself on the verge of a nervous breakdown." Sassoon was consequently sent to Craiglockhart.

Robert Graves married Nancy Nicholson in January 1918 (Wilfred Owen was in attendance) and went on to become the complete man of letters, producing novels, biographies, essays and a vast output of love poetry. In fact, Graves is the living proof that "what will survive of us is love". His relationship with Laura Riding and "the strong pulling of her bladed mind" dominated much of the middle of his life and this is not the place to tell that extraordinary story, except to say that she abandoned him and he settled in Majorca permanently in 1956 with his second wife. He was quite willing to talk about the war years, telling Malcolm Muggeridge (in a wonderfully genial and teasing broadcast double-act from the 1960s) that it was all "marvellous". But he disliked his war poems. There are several that look back to 1914-18: 'Armistice Day', 'A Dedication of Three Hats', 'The Oldest Soldier' and 'Recalling War'. Perhaps Graves is at his best when he looks even further back to a time long before trench warfare was dreamt of, using his historical imagination as he did in his hugely popular novel *I, Claudius*. 'The Legion' (1916) is another kind of twinning: two old soldiers "gulping wine" contemplate the passing troops (we think of ghost legions, perhaps). One is convinced it is the 23rd Legion; the other insists they're "dead, dead, and won't rise again" but what concerns him is the slovenliness of this bunch, as he laments: "O brown cheek, muscled shoulder, sturdy thigh!/ Where are they now?" and his friend reassures him that some things are bigger than the individuals who take part: "The Legion is the Legion while Rome stands/And these same men before the autumn's fall/Shall bang old Vercingetorix out of Gaul." Had Charles Sorley lived, he and Robert Graves might have played the parts of the two old centurions. As Thomas Hardy put it, in 'The Man He Killed', 12 years before the First World War:

> 'Had he and I but met
> By some old ancient inn,
> We should have sat us down to wet
> Right many a nipperkin!'

Instead, as Graves wrote in one of his letters home on hearing of Sorley's death: "what waste!"

Further Reading

Charles Sorley:
Collected Poems (ed. Jean Moorcroft Wilson, Cecil Woolf, 1985)
Out of Battle (ed. Jon Silkin, Routledge and Kegan Paul, 1972)
* * *
Moorcroft Wilson, Jean, *Charles Hamilton Sorley: A Biography* (1985)
Spear, Hilda, (ed.) *Poems and Selected Letters* (Dundee, 1978)

Robert Graves:
Complete Poems (Penguin, 2003)
Goodbye To All That (Cape, 1929)
Poems About War (Cassell, 1988)

10

Key Poems of the First World War

The first poem of the Great War was written five months before it began, by "Thomas Hardy, clairvoyant" as Paul Fussell calls him. 'Channel Firing' is a 74-year-old's wry dramatisation of how he imagines the Wessex dead might react to the sound of "gunnery practice out at sea":

> That night your great guns, unawares,
> Shook all our coffins as we lay,
> And broke the chancel window-squares,
> We thought it was the Judgment-day
>
> And sat upright.

The aural effects ("guns, unawares"), the metrical virtuosity (iambics suddenly disrupted by "Shook all …") and the brilliant enjambment in lines four-five make this poem an arresting opener to any anthology of war poetry, and Andrew Motion wisely puts it on the first page of his invaluable *Poems of the First World War*. Isaac Rosenberg's malevolent God is anticipated ("Ha, ha. It will be warmer when/I blow the trumpet") as is his vision of the "same old druid Time" in the final stanzas:

> Again the guns disturbed the hour,
> Roaring their readiness to avenge,
> As far inland as Stourton Tower,
> And Camelot, and starlit Stonehenge.

Hardy always delighted to show how everything carries on in ironic obliviousness – rather as the *Titanic* and the iceberg are 'constructed' at the same time in 'The Convergence of the Twain'. So, "the glebe cow drools" as usual, Camelot (presumably Cadbury Castle) goes on dreaming of a new set of recruits to its valiant order of heroes and Stonehenge waits for the next wave of human sacrifices. Hardy's 'In the Time of "The Breaking of Nations"', covers similar territory in a more concise form. While the fields of France are to be "torn" (to use Rosenberg's adjective), at home "an old horse that stumbles and nods' carries on ploughing, "though Dynasties pass". It is the 'Theme of Edward Thomas' 'As the Team's Head-Brass'.

Although few were as prescient as Hardy (1840-1928), other Victorian poets responded to the war, notably A.E. Housman (1859-1936), whose *A Shropshire Lad* (1896) was the individual volume most likely to be found in the kit of soldiers at the front. His poems of the Great War are rarely specific, but often go to the heart of the matter, as in this four-line elegy, with its perfectly placed caesura before the final phrase:

> Here dead we lie because we did not choose
>> To live and shame the land from which we sprung.
> Life, to be sure, is nothing much to lose;
>> But young men think it is, and we were young.

His 'Epitaph on an Army of Mercenaries' was apparently his response to German propaganda that claimed the British army were hired mercenaries. The poem reminds us what Larkin learnt from Housman (see particularly his 'Homage to a Government'):

> These, in the day when heaven was falling,
>> The hour when earth's foundations fled,
> Followed their mercenary calling
>> And took their wages and are dead.
>
> Their shoulders held the sky suspended;
>> They stood, and earth's foundations stay;
> What God abandoned, these defended,
>> And saved the sum of things for pay.

Hugh McDiarmid (1892-1978) retorted to the above lines with his own Epitaph, which begins "It is A God-damned lie to say that these/Saved, or knew, anything worth any man's pride./They were professional murderers ..." and one can almost hear his Scots tongue curling around that last word.

Rudyard Kipling (1865-1936), who had heard the guns from further afield than Hardy (the bombardment at Passchendaele was audible in Burwash, Sussex) and who died in the same year as Housman, three years before the Second World War, also made his most significant contribution to the literature of the First in a series of epitaphs. Some of them rival Sassoon in bitterness:

THE BEGINNER

On the first hour of my first day
    In the front trench I fell.
(Children in boxes at a play
    Stand up to watch it well.)

Here, the responsible adults back at home become the childish ones. And this couplet speaks for itself:

COMMON FORM

If any question why we died,
Tell them, because our fathers lied.

Kipling was deeply affected by the death of his son on the Front in 1915 and even Jon Silkin admits that he "responded to certain aspects of the situation with an extraordinary perception". He was, as Lord Derby put it, "the soldiers' poet" and a book of his ballads was equally likely to be in the kitbag. Kipling was invited by Derby to become one of the War Graves Commissioners, and he it was who came up with the inscription that appears in every war cemetery: "Their name liveth for evermore."

But for most readers, First World War Poetry begins with Rugby-and Cambridge-educated Rupert Brooke (1887-1915), the darling of Edward Marsh and the Georgians, the golden thread that links so many of the poets we are considering. As Brian Gardner puts it in

Up the Line to Death: "Suffused with patriotism, he was happy, almost anxious, to die for his country in battle", to purge "a world grown old and cold and weary" ('Peace'). His sonnet 'The Soldier', one from a series of six, was originally called 'The Recruit' and was probably given its present title by Wilfrid Gibson as he prepared it for publication in the journal *New Numbers*. The poem captured a public mood and expressed an idea that had appealed since Thomas Hardy had declared of Drummer Hodge: "portion of that unknown plain/Will Hodge for ever be". It was the same idea that moved Edward Thomas to hold up a fistful of English soil to show what he was literally fighting for. In Brooke's sonnet (Tony Blair's favourite poem, according to *The Big Book of Little Poems*) there is a more imperialistic note to "some corner of a foreign field/That is for ever England". "England" is not quite "Hodge". In death, the simple Wessex Everyman will be alienated and disconcerted by the foreign landscape and different constellations; "England" is still staking her claim, spreading the sweetness and light of her purity into dubious foreign dirt. Ivor Gurney was not impressed, nor was Isaac Rosenberg, but the sonnet's diction does sound a pure note above the "dim land of peace" that Ezra Pound mocked in contemporary poetry and it is certainly preferable to some of the sentiments in his other sonnets: "Now, God be thanked Who has matched us with His hour ..." In 'The Soldier', Brooke repeats "England" and "English" as Rosenberg repeats "wheels" in 'Dead Man's Dump' and the difference speaks volumes. As a sonnet, 'The Soldier' is not quite Shakespearean, not quite Italian: appropriate for a poet who perished neither at home nor in action, but in mid-voyage, on his way to Gallipoli. He contracted blood poisoning and died on St George's Day, 1915, and is buried on Achilles' island, Scyros.

Other significant poems of the early war years include 'Into Battle', by the eldest son of Lord Desborough, Julian Grenfell (1888-1915). This poem has featured in virtually every anthology of First World War literature. The anaphoric opening ("And ... And ... And ...") suggests an urgency, as well as boredom with life. Bernard Bergonzi has shrewdly pointed out that Yossarian, the hero of *Catch 22*, would probably have responded to "And who dies fighting has increase" with "Who dies fighting is dead!". There was a streak of Yossarian in Grenfell, however, which comes out in his less well known 'Prayer for Those on the Staff' and shows him as more than the boorish warmonger some would make him. In fact, many of the 'serious' war poets wrote such light, satirical verse and it is sad that more of it is not anthologised: "O Lord, who mad'st all things to be/ And madest some things very good/Please keep the extra ADC/From horrid scenes and sights of blood". After a privileged upbringing, followed by various clashes with his overbearing mother, Julian Grenfell found that his destiny led him inescapably into the Army. Tonie and Valmai Holt write that he had found "a worthy goal to work towards. For the first time since he was a schoolboy, he had full parental approval."

'Into Battle' presents the earth as predictably life-giving and war as life-affirming, offering hope for "newer birth" in "comradeship" and a "sworded hip". Nature urges him on, rather than mocking as it will in other men's poems, and battle is an old-fashioned "brazen frenzy" in which "the horses show him nobler powers" and no machine gun, barbed wire or tank, no trench, no mud is to be seen. It is a powerful poem, but it conjures the memory of the surreal merry-go-round ridden by cavalry in Richard Attenborough's film of *Oh, What a Lovely War!*, a scene which precedes one showing the bloody, dirty reality of the battlefield. 'Into Battle' was written on 29th April 1915 at the Ypres Salient and published six weeks later on the day that Grenfell died in hospital of a head wound.

There are other poets writing in this manner at the beginning of the war. The aptly named John Freeman (1880-1929) proclaims 'Happy is England Now' and W.N. Hodgson (1893-1916) laments "Ah we have dwelt in Arcady long time" or prays, "Make me a soldier, Lord". Hodgson was killed on the first day of the Somme. That 1st July was the 19th birthday of E.W. Tennant (1897-1916). He did not die for another three months and left behind him some poems that were less 'gung-ho', more focused on what the trenches really involved. The best known are 'Home Thoughts from Laventie' and 'The Mad Soldier'. E.A. Mackintosh, too, (1893-1917) before he was killed at Cambrai, showed distinct promise, and beyond his bagpiping Celtic melancholy is a canny understanding, not so different from Sorley's "chaps/Who are going to die perhaps":

> The pipes in the streets were playing bravely,
> The marching lads went by

With merry hearts and voices singing
My friends marched out to die ...

Robert Nichols (1893-1944) is a more subtle poet than any of these, although Graves in his essay 'Poetry of World War One' is rather disdainful of the way he exaggerated his experiences: he appeared before American audiences as "a crippled warrior", playing up the melodrama in his performances of such pieces as 'Comrades: an episode'. I possess a newspaper cutting from *The Times* , dated 15th December 1916, which must have been cut out by my great-grandparents while my grandfather was at the front with the Royal Field Artillery. It is Robert Nichols' poem, with the rather painterly title, 'Battery Moving Up to a New Position from Rest Camp: Dawn'. A note at the foot of the rough yellow clipping says "Sketched in France, 1915, Written in England, 1916". One can see why this kind of poetry appeared in the newspapers and was cut out by anxious parents, hoping for a glimpse of what was really going on. Owen and Sassoon would hardly have appeared in *The Times* in 1915. The poem is accurate, even disturbing, but not shocking, not horrifying. It will not interfere with the war effort. We are asked to remember the 'sacrifice', are asked to pray for the soldiers. We are not asked awkward questions.

Some of the most difficult questions were being raised by women whose poems were for many years shunted aside "like wrongs hushed up": war poetry was a male preserve. And, after all, the women poets had survived, many of them living on well into the 1960s and 1970s. It was only as they died and the women's movement began to look for neglected figures that their work emerged from beneath the heaps of soldiers' verses. One early discovery was 'The Farmer' by Fredegond Shove (1889-1949), which captures what it must have felt like to live in a land bereft of its men, where only the farmer goes on sowing "the seed in you that earth shall reap,/When they, their countless lives, and all their thoughts,/Lie scattered by the storm: when peace shall come/With stillness, and long shivers, after death." This appeared in the 1965 anthology *Men Who March Away*, and by the late 1980s Martin Stephen's *Never Such Innocence* had many more to offer us: Janet Begbie's untitled poem, "I shouted for blood as I ran, brother,/Till my bayonet pierced your breast ..."; 'Many

Sisters to Many Brothers' by Rose Macaulay (1881-1958) and Helen Mackay's 'Train' stand out in particular. But most of the women's war poems that have now entered the canon emerged from *Scars Upon my Heart*, which Virago published in 1981. A reading of this landmark publication reveals the concerns of those on the Home Front: poems of departure, separation, anxious waiting, sacrifice and personal loss. Grief is expressed most memorably in 'Lamplight' by May W. Cannan (1893-1973), 'Afterwards' by Margaret Postgate Cole (1893-1980) and, of course, Vera Brittain (1896-1970)'s poems, not as fine as her prose memoirs, but sure-footed in 'Perhaps' and 'To My Brother'. It is the opening line of 'To My Brother' that gives Catherine Reilly's anthology its title. *Scars Upon My Heart* includes some predictable religious outpourings and conventional Georgian watercolours, dwelling on the ironies of spring or the associations of falling leaves. And there are, of course, sufficient doses of jingoism even to justify Sassoon's bitter remarks about women's attitudes. The "high zest" of Jessie Pope's gratingly upbeat verse contributions to *Punch* drove Wilfred Owen to dedicate the first draft of 'Dulce Et Decorum Est ' to her. But there are satires in this book, too: S. Gertrude Ford's 'A Fight to the Finish', for example, and a surprising number of poems in which women look at women either critically or enviously. May O'Rourke's 'The Minority: 1917' is a portrait of a flapper "tinkling her silly mirth", one of several poems by women in which their bitterness at society's indifference is palpable. Winifred M. Letts (1882-1971) is positively Hardyesque in her 'Casualty', which begins:

> John Delaney of the Rifles has been shot.
>   A man we never knew,
>   Does it cloud the day for you
>   That he lies among the dead
> Moving, hearing, heeding not?

Against such doses of irony there are many cheerful ballads of home life, of domestic constraints; there is doggerel describing the sweat and toil of war work, such as M. Winifred Wedgwood's 'The VAD Scullery-Maid's Song', for example or even Jessie Pope's own 'War Girls' ("No longer caged and penned up,/They're going to keep their end up/Till the khaki soldier boys come marching back." There are poems of frustrated love and desperate grief and there are some meditations and pronouncements on feminist issues together with more measured speculations about the meaning of war in a broader perspective: 'For a Survivor' by Elizabeth Daryush (1887-1976), 'Peace' by Eleanor Farjeon (1881-1965), Alice Meynell (1847-1922)'s 'Summer in England, 1914' and Iris Tree (1897-1968)'s untitled sonnet, which concludes: "will the fatted gods be gloried yet,/Glutted with gold and dust and empty state,/The incense of our anguish and our sweat?"

Edith Sitwell (1887-1964), meanwhile, who would go on to write her great lament of the Blitz, 'Still Falls the Rain,' sees the whole war as a dance of death:

> We are the dull blind carrion-fly
> That dance and batten. Though God die
> Mad from the horror of the light—
> The light is mad, too, flecked with blood –
> We dance, we dance, each night.

While we tend to think of Edith Sitwell as far removed from the mud and guts of war poetry, it should be remembered that it was she and her brothers who were among the first to want to publish Wilfred Owen, and several of his poems appeared in their anti-Georgian anthology, *Wheels* (1919).

But there is also, in *Scars Upon My Heart,* much actual experience of war, from those poets who were nurses (or VADs), and experienced the worst, then created poems out of what they encountered or using details gleaned from wounded men: Winifred M. Letts' 'Screens' or 'Pluck' by Eva Dobell (1867-1963). And, interestingly, there are some striking attempts to imagine the life of the soldier (notably Lilian M. Anderson's 'Leave in 1917'), even to write in a soldier's voice, as in Sybil Bristowe's 'Over the Top' or the three lines of 'Nothing to Report' by May Herschel-Clarke, which is as good a riposte as any to Sassoon. He might well have envied its razor rhymes:

> One minute we was laughin', me an' Ted,
> The next, he lay beside me grinnin' – dead.
> 'There's nothin' to report', the papers said.

Outstanding among the individual poems by women is May Wedderburn Cannan's MacNeician 'Rouen', whose distinctiveness was recognised first by Philip Larkin. He had included it in his *Oxford Book of Twentieth Century Verse* and in an interview about the compiling of his book, he told Anthony Thwaite (who was himself overwhelmed by the poem) that he had found it "in the Bodleian in the depths of the stacks, and immediately I knew this was something that had to go in. It seemed to me to have all the warmth and idealism of the VADs in the First World War. I find it enchanting." What still enchants is its flawless metre, its refreshingly clear, unselfpitying tone and its attention to the details of place – something Larkin knew about and had put to good use in his own 'MCMXIV'. 'Rouen' is above all a poem of real, felt experience, like May Sinclair (1865-1946)'s excellent 'Field Ambulance in Retreat' which has the authority of D.H. Lawrence in the way the poet handles the free verse, which is some of the best to come out of the war. Indeed, Sinclair's poem is one of the most accomplished in Catherine Reilly's anthology, from its unfussy, precisely captured opening description of "A straight flagged road, laid on the rough earth", to how, "where the piled corn-wagons went, our dripping/Ambulance carries home/ Its red and white harvest from the fields" and finally "the beautiful, desolate Land/Falls back from the intolerable speed of an Ambulance in retreat/On the sacred, dolorous Way."

Parting and Remembrance are the keynotes of women's poetry in the Great War, the former represented most movingly and musically by Nora Bomford's 'Drafts': three ten-line stanzas, blending two quatrains and a final couplet. Despite the odd dubious rhyme (Blighty/ nightie) this has some of the most intelligent and well-crafted writing of the war on issues of sex, which was not on most soldier-poets' minds – or, at any rate, not in Bomford's sense of the word:

> Sex, nothing more, constituent no greater
> Than those which make an eyebrow's slant or fall,
> In origin, sheer accident, which, later,
> Decides the biggest differences of all,
> And, through a war, involves the chance of death
> Against a life of physical normality—
> So dreadfully safe! O, damn the shibboleth
> Of sex! God knows, we've equal personality.

Why should men face the dark while women stay
To live and laugh and meet the sun each day.

Remembrance is at the heart of Eleanor Farjeon's touching elegies for Edward Thomas. Her unconventional sonnet, 'Easter Monday' has a curious history, as related in *Edward Thomas: the Last Four Years*: his final letter was dated 3rd April, six days before the Easter Monday when he would be killed, but there was an extra note dated Easter Sunday. Farjeon writes: "I read with bewilderment those odd sentences the letter begins with: 'I didn't discover the Egg till Easter Monday' – (but Easter Monday was still a week away). 'It was such a lovely morning, Easter Monday' – (but this is still Easter Sunday, this is the eve)."

The note of remembrance is sometimes sounded most convincingly by poets about whom nothing is known, as in 'The Fallen' by Diana Gurney, which seems to hark back to Shakespeare's "Fear no more the heat o' the sun":

Shall we not lay our holly wreath
Here at the foot of this high cross?
We do not know, perhaps a breath
Of our remembering may come
To them at last where they are sleeping,
They are quiet, they are dumb,
No more of mirth, no more of weeping,
Silent Christmas they are keeping;
Ours the sorrow, ours the loss.

But perhaps the most memorable such poem is by the poet of whose sad life we do now know a little, and whose reputation has grown remarkably in recent years: Charlotte Mew (1869-1928). Her output was not great but her few poems of the war are unforgettable. 'The Cenotaph: *September 1919*' in particular, which ends:

God is not mocked and neither are the dead.
For this will stand in our Market-place –
        Who'll sell, who'll buy
        (Will you or I
Lie each to each with the better grace)?
While looking into every busy whore's and huckster's face

As they drive their bargains, is the Face
Of God: and some young, piteous, murdered face.

The men, of course, were to contribute their own poems of
remembrance and disillusionment. 'A Short Poem for Armistice Day'
and in particular 'To a Conscript of 1940' are the wreaths left by
Herbert Read (1893-1968). The latter might be considered a Second
World War poem, but it is rooted in the First. He was in many ways
an arch-Modernist, but here the shade of Owen accompanies that of
Dante as Read recollects his time on the Front. 'To a Conscript of
1940' has the calm of retrospection, the grim plain-spokenness of
one who sees the world repeating its mistakes:

... He turned towards me and I said:
"I am one of those who went before you
Five-and-twenty years ago: one of the many who never returned,
Of the many who returned and yet were dead.

We went where you are going, into the rain and the mud;
We fought as you will fight
With death and darkness and despair;
We gave what you will give – our brains and our blood ..."

Beside these memorial offerings, Read's 400-line poem 'The End of
a War' is a veritable Menin Gate. Like many long poems, this one
has tended to be overlooked, but it is worth seeking out in Read's
Collected Poems or in W.B. Yeats' *Oxford Book of Modern Verse*.
Yeats famously had no truck with the "passive suffering" of Owen,
but he was clearly impressed with Read. 'The End of a War' consists
of an extended meditation from the perspective of a dying German
officer; a dialogue between the body and soul of a war victim (this is
probably what appealed to Yeats); and finally the thoughts of an
English officer as he wakes to find it is Armistice Day. Read's four-
part sequence 'My Company' is also a distinguished poem of
camaraderie and endurance in which "My men, my modern Christs,/
Your bloody agony confronts the world" and there are other popular
anthology pieces, such as 'The Happy Warrior', a pithy answer to
Wordsworth's question of 1807, "Who is the Happy Warrior? Who
is he/That every man should wish to be?"

Herbert Read was associated with the Imagists, although he never quite became 'one of them' and is not in the standard Penguin anthology. Ford Madox Ford (1873-1939), too, was on the fringes of the movement and while it is his tetralogy of novels, *Parade's End*, that shows him at his best, he was no mean poet and writes with a refreshing directness: Martin Seymour-Smith called his work "genuinely modest, charming and (like most things he did) unusual" while Jon Silkin devotes several pages to him in *Out of Battle*. Basil Bunting edited a selection of his work. This, from his sequence 'Antwerp', highlights both the strengths and weaknesses:

These are the women of Flanders.
They await the lost.
They await the lost that shall never leave the dock;
They await the lost that shall never again come by the train
To the embraces of all these women with dead faces;
They await the lost who lie dead in trench and barrier and foss,
In the dark of the night.
This is Charing Cross; it is past one of the clock;
There is very little light.

There is so much pain.

The most prominent of the card-carrying Imagists to write of the war was Richard Aldington (1892-1962) – although D.H. Lawrence (1885-1930) and F.S.Flint (1885-1960) each left poems (Flint's 'Soldiers' and 'Hats', for instance, or Lawrence's 'Bombardment'). Following the Imagist formula, going "in fear of abstraction" and using "either no ornament or good ornament", Aldington wrote sharply and brightly, though not particularly memorably. 'Field Manoeuvres: Outpost Duty' begins:

The long autumn grass under my body
Soaks my clothes with its dew;
Where my knees press into the ground
I can feel the damp earth ...

Such unmusical verse comes perilously close to chopped-up prose, even in well-known poems such as 'In the Trenches' and while Adrian

Barlow makes a good case for him in *Six Poets of the Great War,* read in bulk, his poetry seems just too skeletal and vapid.

At the opposite end of the spectrum from the Imagists there is the sprawling epic of the war, *In Parenthesis,* published in 1937 by David Jones (1895-1974), with its symphonic interweaving of myth and modernism, dialogue, prose and lyric. This is above all language made into music and, as someone said of Wagner, *In Parenthesis* has wonderful moments but interminable half-hours. Yet there is always a sense of purpose. This is the vernacular of High Modernism: a novelist struggling out of the mud of *The Waste Land* in search of an audience, playing with language, tossing a myth, feeling his way into a new age:

> The repeated passing back of aidful messages assumes a cadency.
> Mind the hole
> mind the hole
> mind the hole to left
> hole right
> step over
> keep left, left.
>   One grovelling, precipitated, with his gear tangled, struggles to feet again:
> Left be buggered.
>   Sorry mate – you all right china? – lift us yer rifle – an' don't take on so Honey – but rather, mind
> the wire here
> mind the wire
> mind the wire
> mind the wire.
>   Extricate with some care that taut strand—it may well be you'll sweat on its unbrokenness.
>   (PART 3: *Starlight Order*)

Then there is Edgell Rickword (1898-1982) who does not really fit into any category, and who is known more these days for his left-wing political sympathies and his essays – because he gave up writing (mainly lyric) verse in his thirties. He had already produced distinctive war poems in 'Trench Poets', the sonnet 'War and Peace' and 'Moonrise' and produced one of the best poems of the war in 'Winter Warfare': "Colonel Cold strode up the line ...", this, his best-known poem begins. It is in a simple Brechtian ballad form and Rickword uses a nicely alliterative personification to point out (as Owen does by very different and less economical means) that freezing weather is just as treacherous whichever side you are on. Whether it is Colonel Cold or Hauptmann Kälte who "stiffened all that met his glare" and "left them burning", it is all the same to the men in the trenches. The poem's success lies in its ingenuity: the parallels between the effect of a severe frost and the effect of a visit by an officer are all so apt. The frostbitten, bullied men in the line can only watch "with hoary eyes" and go on being "torn by screaming steel".

Thousands of men and women were writing poetry while the First World War was happening. Some, like Harold Monro (1879-1932) who so influenced Owen, barely touched on the war except indirectly or through the smokescreen of their own preoccupations. Others wrote using direct and very specific knowledge, like Jeffrey Day (1896-1918), one of the few pilot poets of the war, whose 'On the Wings of the Morning' is well known among RAF fliers even today. The number of poetry collections published from 1914 onwards is staggering and many of the best known journals, *Punch* in particular, made a feature of such verse. The writers of the day all felt that they should have their say, poets or not, so there are often poems attached to names we might have come to associate with other genres: John Galsworthy and Saki and A.A. Milne and G.K. Chesterton. A.P. Herbert (1890-1971) is given particular prominence in Martin Stephen's *Never Such Innocence*, and his poems do have a polish and intelligence that raises them above the level of light verse. Other popular poets, like 'Woodbine Willy', preferred their anonymity: he was, in fact, Geoffrey Kennedy, a padre who donated all his profits to charity and whose books (as Stephen says) were either "bought by soldiers who knew the truth about the war or civilians who thought that in Woodbine Willy they were reading it". Martin Stephen also highlights what he calls one of the "great neglected classics of the war" by Major Owen Rutter (1889-1944), who wrote under the pseudonym of Klip-Klip. 'The Song of Tiadatha' ('Tired Arthur') is certainly more than just another deft parody of Longfellow:

… Then they took him round their trenches,
Round their muddy maze of trenches,
Rather like an aggravated

Rabbit warren with the roof off,
Worse to find one's way about in
Than the dark and windy subways
Of the Piccadilly tube are ...

Thus, many of the keenest voices are or were nameless. Les Murray
includes the following in his *New Oxford Book of Australian Verse*
from the diary of an Australian soldier in September 1917:

Adieu, the years are a broken song,
And the right grows weak in the strife with wrong,
The lilies of love have a crimson stain
And the old days never will come again.

The ballads and marching songs, parodies of music hall numbers
and romantic ditties that bring to *Oh, What a Lovely War!* what
Wilfred Owen brought to Britten's *War Requiem* seldom come with
a name under them. Andrew Motion includes in his *First World War
Poems* several such verses, unexpurgated. They are still catchy: "I
don't want to be a soldier", "For You but Not for Me", not to mention
"Do your balls hang low?", which Haig happened to overhear being
sung by a passing battalion and its commander. Haig complimented
him on his voice and offered a mild rebuke, but as he was leaving, a
voice was heard to start up with: "After the ball is over ...". Edward
Thomas used to sing such army songs with his friends "with a
mischievous quietness" (Gordon Bottomley) and Robert Graves
appeared on television's *Late Night Line-up* and sang 'Hanging on
the Old Barbed Wire' (which officers tried to suppress as it was
considered bad for morale), agreeing with his interviewer that it was
indeed poetry and that "they meant it". There are many such songs
gathered in Max Arthur's *When This Bloody War Is Over*. As Lyn
Macdonald says in her substantial introduction, "The songs are still
remembered, and some still sung almost a century after the start of
that 'Great War' that still haunts succeeding generations."

Another source of anonymous verse was the newspapers produced
by different regiments, the most famous of which was the *Wipers
Times.* In the Christmas 1916 issue of the 23rd Division's magazine,
The Dump, we find a variety of wittily turned limericks:

There was a young man at Armentières
Who went to his work with a jaunty air.
'For,' he said, 'it is clear
That the atmosphere here
Is healthier than the Laventie air.'

And in the 5th Gloster Magazine of February 1917, there is even a parody of W.B. Yeats:

I will arise and go now and go to Picardy
And a new trench line hold there, of clay and shell-holes made.
No dug-outs shall I have there, nor a hive for the Lewis G
But live on top in the b. loud glade.

Meanwhile, Yeats himself had made his contribution from a safe distance with 'An Irish Airman Foresees his Death', and various references in *The Wild Swans at Coole*, including 'On Being Asked for a War Poem' which opens, "I think it better that in times like these/A poet's mouth be silent ..." Other less well known Irishmen were actually at the Front Line: Patrick MacGill's 'The Star-shell *(Loos)*' begins: "A star-shell holds the sky beyond/Shell-shivered Loos ...", which is where he was wounded and thereafter largely forgotten. Francis Ledwidge is a different case. He is barely a war poet at all, but undoubtedly a poet of the war. While he was at the Front, he composed those few lyrics that do refer to the action, just half a dozen in the final section of his *Complete Poems*. Ledwidge (1887-1917) was killed in Flanders – a death which he seems, like Yeats' airman, to foresee in the last stanza of 'Soliloquy':

... It is too late now to retrieve
A fallen dream, too late to grieve
A name unmade, but not too late
To thank the gods for what is great;
A keen-edged sword, a soldier's heart,
Is greater than a poet's art.
And greater than a poet's fame
A little grave that has no name,
Whence honour turns away in shame.

James Stephens thought Ledwidge had more promise than any poet of the period; and Seamus Heaney has since championed the work of what he called "an unusually sensitive, tenacious and tormented nature", commemorating him in *Field Work* (1979) with 'In Memoriam Francis Ledwidge':

... I think of you in your Tommy's uniform
A haunted Catholic face, pallid and brave,
Ghosting the trenches with a bloom of hawthorn
Or silence cored from a Boyne passage-grave ...

The Australian Les Murray, in turn, has rediscovered the poetry of Harley Matthews (1889-1968) for his *New Oxford Book of Australian Verse*. The best Australian poet of the war is usually considered to be Frederic Manning (1882-1935), for poems such as 'The Trenches', which powerfully evokes the life of the men "goaded like the damned by some invisible wrath,/A will stronger than weariness, stronger than animal fear,/Implacable and monotonous." But Harley Matthews was elsewhere: he survived the Anzac landings at Gallipoli and published a slim volume of 'story-poems' about the experience in the 1930s. The best of them is 'Women Are Not Gentlemen', which tells of a sniper in Gallipoli whom the troops, with predictable consequences, believed to be female:

Deep in the hush somewhere
A rifle whispers, a spent bullet whirs
Past us. "That is not hers.
It is too early for her yet ..."

While the Western Front has had its fair share of poets, Gallipoli has fewer, but this and Sidney Powell (1878-1952)'s 17-page 'Gallipoli' to some extent redress the balance. Martin Stephen includes a substantial extract from the Powell in his anthology. There is also Geoffrey Dearmer, born the same year as Owen, and whose uplifting verses about his experience in the Dardanelles (and the trenches) were published for his hundredth birthday in 1993.

Of the Canadians involved in the war, it was Robert Service (1874-1958), "the man with the ice in his voice" whose lines most readily tripped from the well-oiled tongues of "the poor bloody infantry" after the war. But there was also the doctor John McCrae (1872-1918) who is celebrated for one poem: 'In Flanders Fields', written during the Second Battle of Ypres. As Paul Fussell says, this poem "manages to accumulate the maximum number of well-known motifs and images", even culminating in the trusty torch handed on from Henry Newbolt's 'Vitae Lampada'. It was 'In Flanders Fields' that inspired the British Legion to take the poppy as its symbol of remembrance after an American YMCA worker, Moina Michael, read the poem and came up with one of her own in which she suggests wearing "the Poppy red ... in honour of our dead". The most accomplished of her countrymen involved in the fighting was Alan Seeger (1888-1916), who came to the war via the French Foreign Legion. "I have a rendezvous with Death" is his most quoted line. The rendezvous occurred on American Independence Day in 1916 on the Somme.

The American Ezra Pound (1885-1972), of course, did not fight but he produced in 'Hugh Selwyn Mauberley' what is in many ways the most succinct commentary on the war, its motives ("fear of weakness ... love of slaughter in imagination") its consequences, its futility ("non 'dulce' non 'et decor'"). He deliberately uses his friend Binyon's favourite "myriad", holding it up briefly like a decoration, only to smash and sully it with "bitch" and "botched".

There died a myriad,
And of the best, among them,
For an old bitch gone in the teeth,
For a botched civilization...

Further Reading

Arthur, Max, (ed.) *When This Bloody War is Over* (Piatkus, 2001)
Barlow, (ed.) *Six Poets of the Great War* (inc. Aldington) (CUP, 1995)
Gardner, Brian, (ed.) *Up the Line to Death* (Methuen, 1964)
Jones, (ed.) *Imagist Poetry* (Penguin, 1972)
Littlewood/Raffles and company, *Oh What a Lovely War!* (Methuen, 1967)
Motion, Andrew, (ed.) *First World War Poems* (Faber, 2003)
Murray, (ed.) *New Oxford Book of Australian Verse* (OUP, 1986)

Parsons, (ed.) *Men Who March Away* (Heinemann, 1965)

Powell, Anne, (ed.) *A Deep Cry* (Sutton, 1998)

Reilly, Catherine (ed.) *Scars Upon My Heart* (Virago, 1981)

Silkin, Jon, (ed.) *The Penguin Book of First World War Poetry*

Stephen, Martin, (ed.) *Never Such Innocence* (Everyman, 1991)

Yeats, (ed.) *Oxford Book of Modern Verse* (OUP, 1936)
Dearmer:

Stallworthy, (ed.) *A Pilgrim's Song* (selected poems)

11

The Lattermath

What of the lattermath to this hoar Spring?
Edward Thomas ('It was upon …')

In his 1965 review of *Men Who March Away,* Ted Hughes described the First World War as our "national ghost" and France as "England's dream world, a previously unguessed fantasy dimension, where the social oppressions and corruptions slipped into nightmare gear". It is true that the events of 1914-18 have obsessed English writers and writers in English more enduringly even than the inhumanities of the Second World War. In this brief chapter, I wish to alert readers to the work of those poets who have put this war near the centre of their preoccupations and others who have turned to it and produced memorable individual poems.

Ted Hughes (1930-1998) could have been speaking of himself when he suggested that we are haunted by the Great War. It has been central to Hughes' poetry since his first collection, *The Hawk in the Rain* (1957), whose last few pages introduce three poems which look back to that era: 'Bayonet Charge', with its characteristic nightmare opening "Suddenly he awoke and was running— "; the triptych of sonnets, 'Griefs for Dead Soldiers', which should be better known for its attention to a bereaved wife's view of events: "She cannot build her sorrow into a monument/And walk away from it"; and the well known 'Six Young Men', one of many contemporary poems about the war which use a photograph as a starting point. Hughes was fascinated by the fact that Wilfred Owen carried photographs of battlefield horrors with him to show those at home who seemed to him too complacent and he had a plan to exhibit enlargements of them in London. 'Wilfred Owen's Photographs' from *Lupercal* (1960) indirectly refers to this. Hughes suggests in his review that Owen's poems are "partly substitutes or verbal parallels for those photographs".

Hughes' father had occasionally told stories about the war when he was young, but became increasingly silent, a fact which pervades the poems about him: "My father sat in his chair recovering/From the four-year mastication by gunfire and mud,/Body buffeted wordless ..." ('Out', *Wodwo*, 1967): "My post-war father was so silent/He seemed to be listening" ('Dust as We Are'). This latter poem is from *Wolfwatching* (1989), the book in which Hughes broke his own extended silence about his father and turned back from mythological topics to human ones, most memorably in 'For the Duration', which begins: "I felt a strange fear when the war-talk,/Like a creeping barrage, approached you." What haunted William Hughes was the knowledge that he was one of only 17 in his regiment who had survived Gallipoli, as suggested in 'The Last of the 1st/5th Lancashire Fusiliers', subtitled 'a Souvenir of the Gallipoli Landings'. The facts about trench warfare came more from Ted's uncle Walt, who is also commemorated in *Wolfwatching* and the earlier uncollected 'My Uncle's Wound'. But as Elaine Feinstein points out in her life of the poet, "Men from every part of the valley had died in those battlefields", and this truth shadows *Remains of Elmet* (1979), with its evocation of "First, mills and steep wet cobbles/Then cenotaphs" of "the melting corpses of farms/The hills' skulls peeled by the dragging climate" and "A land naked now as a wound/That the sun swabs and dabs//Where the miles of agony are numbness/And harebell and heather a euphoria." Interestingly, in the light of his remarks about the equivalent power of photography, these poems first appeared alongside a series of dark, brooding monochrome images of the Calder Valley taken by Fay Godwin.

It is this capacity to inject a scene or a story with the imagery and emotions of the First World War that is so typical of Hughes. Even the bitterly sardonic mood of his controversial sequence *Crow* (1970) seems indebted to the period and individual poems about animals draw their imagery "red in tooth and claw" from it. One of the best is 'Tiger-Psalm' from the collection *Moortown* (1979), which contrasts the way a tiger kills ("Does not kill. The tiger blesses with a fang.") with the methods of the First World War, taking Owen's "rapid rattle" to its logical conclusion and making the words sound like something pattering out of a computer, a cold, calculating abuse of the brain's left lobe:

> The tiger
> Kills
> With the strength of five tigers, kills exalted.
> The machine-guns
> Permit themselves a snigger. They eliminate the error
> With a to-fro dialectic
> And the point proved stop speaking.

In his somewhat obscure Laureate poem, 'A Masque for Three Voices', Ted Hughes confesses, as he writes of how "Passchendaele and Somme disturb me more" (than Agincourt or Trafalgar): "I only know what ghosts breathe in my breath – /The shiver of their battles my Shibboleth."

The other contemporary poet who has returned compulsively to themes of the First World War is the Ulsterman, Michael Longley (born 1939) whose latest collection *Snow Water* (2004) includes a sequence of 10 poems set mainly in the trenches and who even felt able to gather 60 of his war poems into *Cenotaph of Snow* (Enitharmon, 2003). In introducing it, he calls himself "a non-combatant drawn to the subject of war" by the fact that his father fought in both the First and Second World Wars, by his own reverence for "Owen, Rosenberg, Sassoon, Sorley, Blunden, Thomas, Jones and their successors of 1939-1918", by a love of Homer's "most powerful of all war poems", the *Iliad,* and by seeing his native Ulster "disfigured for thirty years by fratricidal violence". He does not mention the influence of his wife, the formidable critic Edna Longley, who has made the poetry of war a special study, writing particularly persuasively on Edward Thomas (see *Poetry in the Wars* and her edition of Thomas' prose, *A Language Not to be Betrayed*).

As with Hughes, Longley's best known poems of the Great War focus on his father, "a belated casualty" poisoned by "lead traces", "dying for King and Country, slowly". 'In Memoriam' from his first collection is less well known than 'Wounds' from his second. This has been much anthologised, a poem impressive for its candour as well as for its bold shifts of perspective. Again, the memory is set unreeling by images that appear like photographs:

Here are two pictures from my father's head—
I have kept them like secrets until now:

And they are as shocking as anything Wilfred Owen might have wanted to show, because here is ineradicable bigotry and hatred of an enemy who is not in the opposite trench at all, and has (to the poet's father's "admiration and bewilderment") nothing to do with what is about to kill these young men:

First, the Ulster Division at the Somme
Going over the top with "Fuck the Pope!"
"No Surrender!": a boy about to die,
Screaming "Give 'em one for the Shankill!"

The second picture is equally bizarre in its way, of a "London-Scottish padre" adjusting kilts in "a landscape of dead buttocks". The poem then shifts to the victims and volunteers on the latterday battlefield in Ulster: young men once again, "teenage soldiers, bellies full of/ Bullets" and "a shivering boy" who apologises weakly to the children and "a bewildered wife" as he shoots her husband in his carpet slippers.

Other Longley poems remembering the First War include family anecdotes ('Master of Ceremonies' and 'Second Sight') but there are some which take a broader, longer look as in 'The War Graves':

… The headstones wipe out the horizon like a blizzard
And we can see no farther than the day they died,
As though all of them died together on the same day
And the war was that single momentous explosion...

(*The Weather in Japan*, 2000)

This (for Longley) long poem culminates in a consideration of graves of the poets of the war and there are many other shorter ones that focus on these writers that he so reveres: 'The War Poets', 'No Man's Land: *in memory of Isaac Rosenberg*', and several about Edward Thomas ranging from two from the mid-1970s in *Man Lying on a Wall* ('Edward Thomas' War Diary' and 'Mole') to a group in his recent collection *The Weather in Japan*: 'The Moustache' compares Thomas in his attempts "to cover up/His aesthete's features" with Longley's own father "aged twenty, in command of a company/Who,

120

because most of them shaved only once a week/And some not at all, were known as Longley's Babies." Another, titled simply 'Poetry', picks up on some of those coincidences and synchronicities which are so fascinating in the lives of the period. 'Poetry' relates unaffectedly (in 14 unrhymed lines) how "when he was billeted in a ruined house in Arras" Blunden found what he thought might be Thomas' own copy of his book about Keats, and how "When Thomas Hardy died his widow gave Blunden/As a memento of many visits to Max Gate/His treasured copy of Edward Thomas' *Poems*."

Michael Longley is by no means alone in his fascination with Edward Thomas, who could be seen as the presiding spirit of post-war English verse – were so many of his fans not from corners of foreign fields. Longley is just one of innumerable contributors to *Elected Friends: Poems for and about Edward Thomas* (ed. Anne Harvey, Enitharmon, 1991). Glyn Maxwell's enigmatic 'Letters to Edward Thomas' had not been written when this fine anthology appeared, but would surely have found a place alongside the contribution from his teacher, Derek Walcott. Of the poets born since the Second World War, who can only have heard talk of the war from their grandfathers, Glyn Maxwell (born 1962) stands out as one peculiarly drawn to the events, notably in his 1998 Faber collection, *The Breakage*, which includes the Thomas sequence and a cluster of war poems: 'England Germany' describes a football match as if it were the war, 'Valentines at the Front' imagines the incongruity of white and pink love tokens in the trenches, while 'June 31st, The Somme' is a particularly successful exploration of the way men would play with time when waiting for an attack. The poem enters Paul Fussell's twilight zone, where "dawn was like a dusk" so you could fool yourself "a day could never/Quite break/On the First". Time shifts forward at the end of the poem to a room prepared for a new child. Glyn Maxwell is surely not alone in feeling how uncanny it is that his very existence comes down to the chance behaviour of bullets and shrapnel.

Again it is a photograph that prompts one of *The Breakage*'s best poems (it features on the cover) 'My Grandfather at the Pool'. With a conscious nod to Ted Hughes in 'Six Young Men', Maxwell sees this group of five and notes that "The only one who turned away is him,/About to live the trenches and survive,/Alone, as luck would have it, of the five." Like Hughes in 'Walt' ("Here," he hazarded.

"Somewhere just about here."), Maxwell is moved by the old soldier's need to pin down a precise location, and the neat couplets are for a moment disrupted:

> I narrow my own eyes until they blur.
> In a blue sneeze of a cornfield near Flers
>
> In 1969, he went. *Near here*
>
> *It happened* and he didn't say it twice.
> It's summer and the pool will be like ice.
>
> Five pals in Liverpool about to swim.
> The only one who looks away is him.

One of the boldest responses to the First World War was published in 1996 by John Gurney (1935-2000). *War* is a 16,000 line blank verse epic written from the point of view of an aviator (Gurney himself was a fighter pilot) exploring the apparently "civilised and clean" life of airmen "compared with our unholy infantry". What makes it unusual, apart from its length and its lack of almost everything that a volume of contemporary poetry needs to succeed, is its sheer scope and the fact that it explores an area which fascinated the wartime generation, yet has been quietly shunted aside: the occult. Gurney knows full well the popularity of Sir Oliver Lodge's best-selling 1916 book about his conversations with his son, Raymond, killed at the Front. He knows how many people were consulting mediums. He knows, too, like Graves, that the Front certainly felt like a haunted place. The narrator of *War*, a neurasthenic squadron-major, is also a medium and spends many of his non-flying hours in conversation with William Blake, visiting different spiritual planes. Although there is a strong narrative to Gurney's 24-book epic, building to the climactic single combat between the narrator and the German ace, Von Streich, at *War*'s heart is a mythic quest through the unconscious for the sources of evil. As the narrator searches for his newly-dead and spiritually scarred brother, we witness the complex structure of the afterlife, its many hazards, but also the various opportunities for healing; and we are shown "the great task", which is (as Gurney has Blake put it) "to introvert all war".

The Mystery of the Charity of Charles Péguy (1983) by Geoffrey Hill (born 1932) is a miniature by comparison – a mere 400 lines – and it circles more conventional landmarks of religion and philosophy surrounding the life of Charles Péguy, who died in a beetroot field on the first day of the Battle of the Marne in September 1914. Hill's evocation of the war in the early stanzas is not easily forgotten. Once more, it is photography (or, in this case, cinematography) that provides the adequate image and Hill has chosen pararhyme to provide an apt soundtrack:

> Violent contrariety of men and days; calm
> juddery bombardment of a silent film
> showing such things: its canvas slashed with rain
> and St Elmo's fire. Victory of the machine!
>
> The brisk celluloid clatters through the gate;
> the cortège of the century dances in the street;
> and over and over the jolly cartoon
> armies of France go reeling towards Verdun.

Some of the contemporary poets who have returned in their work to this particular nightmare landscape are those who have experienced war at first hand, such as Charles Causley or Vernon Scannell, whose recent *New and Selected Poems* opens with several impressive additions to the muster. Other names are familiar as editors or critics: so, Jon Silkin (who wrote a play about Gurney), P.J. Kavanagh (particularly for 'Edward Thomas in Heaven'), Andrew Motion for his long poem 'Joe Soap' (in *The Price of Everything*) and Jon Stallworthy for his anthology set-piece 'No Ordinary Sunday'. One might expect David Constantine (b.1944), with his scholarly understanding of German culture, to find an original angle – and so he does, but in his best war poem it is by attending to the effect of loss on "the wife, the mother/ Or any beloved woman", a topic largely overlooked by male writers. The nine-part sequence, 'In Memoriam 8571 Private J.W. Gleave' was written for his grandfather, killed on the Somme and his grandmother who survived him by half a century:

> How soon, I wonder, after how many Novembers
> Did the years begin to seem not paces
> Interminably around a pit nor steps deserting

> A place, but slow degrees by which she came
> Over the curve of the world into that hemisphere
> His face rose in? ...
>
> (from *Part 2*)

Constantine achieves a formal clarity, a vibratoless purity of tone, which is lofty without becoming portentous. Perhaps this was, after all, learnt from the German – Hölderlin, whom he has translated, or even late Beethoven.

There are some who have produced just one landmark commentary, such as Larkin's threnody, 'MCMXIV', which captures with photographic accuracy both the nostalgic gaiety of that last summer and the inescapable fate awaiting those "moustached archaic faces/ Grinning as if it were all/An August Bank Holiday lark". Only Larkin (1922-1985) would think to remark on "the countryside not caring" or the "differently-dressed servants/With tiny rooms in huge houses":

> Never such innocence,
> Never before or since,
> As changed itself to past
> Without a word—the men
> Leaving the gardens tidy,
> The thousands of marriages,
> Lasting a little while longer:
> Never such innocence again.

Another Hull poet, Sean O'Brien (born 1952), opens his 1987 collection *The Frighteners* in the post-innocence world, 'In a Military Archive'. Writing of the "grave-geographies/Of Arras, Albert and Thiepval" he remarks how "Now literature is sent, as once/Were razor-blades and letters,/That the dead may study suffering/In the language of their betters." A similar tone permeates the work of Tony Harrison (born 1937), particularly his BBC film poem 'The Gaze of the Gorgon' (1992), in which the Kaiser himself features, supervising the excavation of a Gorgon's head in Corfu:

> The scholar Kaiser on the scent
> of long lost temple pediment
> not filling trenches, excavating
> the trenches where the Gorgon's waiting
> there in the trench to supervise

the unearthing of the Gorgon's eyes.

This move from the trenches of the battlefields to the trenches of an archaeological dig is perhaps an apt analogy for the way poets now write about the First World War: digging into the past, brushing off artefacts and heirlooms, excavating stories, images, facts. Just as the fields of the Somme still generate tons of munitions each year, so 1914-1918 is by no means an exhausted field for contemporary writers. Among recent unexpected contributors to the literature of the Great War are Susan Wicks (born 1947) who has just published (with Bloodaxe Books, like Harrison and O'Brien) a series of poems about Flanders, "our songs translating themselves/into mud, into tree-skeletons,/craters where the bodies of birds/lay bleeding" and the Australian, Les Murray (born 1938) whose picaresque verse novel *Fredy Neptune* (1998), about a man who loses the sense of touch, has much to say about some of the less well documented action of the war:

> … God, I'm putting off remembering
> or telling this part. Farah Gorge. The Nine Miles of Dead.
> In Egypt I'd been spared seeing it. Arrested and hung
> I'd have been spared it. The War at last, as I'd avoided seeing it.
> The pilots were all sickened. I'm not sure there were orders I
> should see it
> nor permission to take me. They needed me to see it
> and not to see it. Two army corps, trapped hopeless in a
> steep gorge,
>
> a traffic jam made with bombs and guns at each end
> then butchered at leisure. The Turks had been retreating from
> Nablus
> down to the Jordan. You can't take surrenders from the air,
> so the orders were: Destroy them. Day after bloody day, packed
> thousands,
> anything standing, lay it out, anything still moving, nail it …

Paul Muldoon's 'Truce', Douglas Dunn's 'Portrait Photograph, 1915', Lotte Kramer's 'Anecdote 1920s, Rhineland' and Anne Stevenson's 'Sarajevo, June 28, 1914' would all have a place in any anthology of contemporary poems of the Great War – the work of Irish, Scottish, Anglo-German and Anglo-American poets respectively. Ted Hughes may have been right about the "national ghost", but the exorcising of it may require something of an international effort. Or it may be that time will do the trick, as it will eventually have reduced the last shell in No Man's Land to red dust. It is likely that a generation of poets that cannot remember grandparents talking (or not talking) about 1914-1918 will find nothing there to move them to poetry. On the other hand, it may be that the greatest poem of the Great War has yet to be written. Whatever the case, just as there will always be wars, there will always be poets to warn. All the rest of us can do today is read them.

Further Reading

David Constantine:
Selected Poems (Bloodaxe, 1991)
John Gurney:
War (Salzburg University Press, 1996)
Tony Harrison:
The Gaze of the Gorgon (Bloodaxe, 1992)
Geoffrey Hill:
The Mystery of the Charity of Charles Péguy (Agenda Editions, 1983)
Ted Hughes:
Keegan, (ed.) *Collected Poems* (Faber, 2003)
The Hawk in the Rain (Faber, 1957)
Wolfwatching (Faber, 1989)
Scammell, (ed.) *Winter Pollen* (Faber, 1994)
Michael Longley:
Cenotaph of Snow: 60 Poems About War (Enitharmon, 2003)
Poems 1963-1983 (Secker, 1991)
Selected poems (Cape, 1998)
Snow Water (Cape, 2004)
The Weather in Japan (Cape, 2000)
Glyn Maxwell:
The Breakage (Faber, 1998)
Les Murray:
Vernon Scannell, *Of Love and War* (Robson, 2002)
Fredy Neptune (Carcanet, 1998)
Susan Wicks:
Night Toad (Bloodaxe, 2003)

GREENWICH EXCHANGE BOOKS

Greenwich Exchange Student Guides are critical studies of major or contemporary serious writers in English and selected European languages. The series is for the student, the teacher and 'common readers' and is an ideal resource for libraries. The *Times Educational Supplement* praised these books, saying, "The style of these guides has a pressure of meaning behind it. Students should learn from that ... If art is about selection, perception and taste, then this is it."

(ISBN prefix 1-871551- applies)
The series includes:
W.H. Auden by Stephen Wade (36-6)
Honoré de Balzac by Wendy Mercer (48-X)
William Blake by Peter Davies (27-7)
The Brontës by Peter Davies (24-2)
Robert Browning by John Lucas (59-5)
Samuel Taylor Coleridge by Andrew Keanie (64-1) .
Joseph Conrad by Martin Seymour-Smith (18-8)
William Cowper by Michael Thorn (25-0)
Charles Dickens by Robert Giddings (26-9)
Emily Dickinson by Marnie Pomeroy (68-4)
John Donne by Sean Haldane (23-4)
Ford Madox Ford by Anthony Fowles (63-3)
The Stagecraft of Brian Friel by David Grant (74-9)
Robert Frost by Warren Hope (70-6)
Thomas Hardy by Sean Haldane (33-1)
Seamus Heaney by Warren Hope (37-4)
Gerard Manley Hopkins by Sean Sheehan (77-3)
James Joyce by Michael Murphy (73-0)
Philip Larkin by Warren Hope (35-8)
Poets of the First World War by John Greening (79-X)
Laughter in the Dark – The Plays of Joe Orton by Arthur Burke (56-0)
Philip Roth by Paul McDonald (72-2)
Shakespeare's *Macbeth* by Matt Simpson (69-2)
Shakespeare's *Othello* by Matt Simpson (71-4)
Shakespeare's *The Tempest* by Matt Simpson (75-7)
Shakespeare's Non-Dramatic Poetry by Martin Seymour-Smith (22-6)
Shakespeare's Sonnets by Martin Seymour-Smith (38-2)
Tobias Smollett by Robert Giddings (21-8)
Dylan Thomas by Peter Davies (78-1)
Alfred, Lord Tennyson by Michael Thorn (20-X)
William Wordsworth by Andrew Keanie (57-9)

OTHER GREENWICH EXCHANGE BOOKS
Paperback unless otherwise stated.

LITERATURE & BIOGRAPHY

Aleister Crowley and the Cult of Pan *by Paul Newman*
Few more nightmarish figures stalk English literature than Aleister Crowley (1875-1947), poet, magician, mountaineer and agent provocateur. In this groundbreaking study, Paul Newman dives into the occult mire of Crowley's works and fishes out gems and grotesqueries that are by turns ethereal, sublime, pornographic and horrifying. An influential exponent of the cult of the Great God Pan, his essentially 'pagan' outlook was shared by major European writers as well as English novelists like E.M. Forster, D.H. Lawrence and Arthur Machen.
Paul Newman lives in Cornwall. Editor of the literary magazine *Abraxas*, he has written over ten books.
2004 • 223 pages • ISBN 1-871551-66-8

The Author, the Book and the Reader *by Robert Giddings*
This collection of essays analyses the effects of changing technology and the attendant commercial pressures on literary styles and subject matter. Authors covered include Charles Dickens, Tobias George Smollett, Mark Twain, Dr Johnson and John le Carré.
1991 • 220 pages • illustrated • ISBN 1-871551-01-3

John Dryden *by Anthony Fowles*
Of all the poets of the Augustan age, John Dryden was the most worldly. Anthony Fowles traces Dryden's evolution from 'wordsmith' to major poet. This critical study shows a poet of vigour and technical panache whose art was forged in the heat and battle of a turbulent polemical and pamphleteering age. Although Dryden's status as a literary critic has long been established, Fowles draws attention to Dryden's neglected achievements as a translator of poetry. He deals also with the less well-known aspects of Dryden's work – his plays and occasional pieces.
Anthony Fowles was born in London and educated at the Universities of Oxford and Southern California. He began his career in filmmaking before becoming an author of film and television scripts and more than twenty books.
2003 • 292 pages • ISBN 1-871551-58-7

The Good That We Do *by John Lucas*
John Lucas' book blends fiction, biography and social history in order to tell the story of his grandfather, Horace Kelly. Headteacher of a succession of elementary schools in impoverished areas of London, 'Hod' Kelly was also a keen cricketer, a devotee of the music hall, and included among his friends the great Trade Union leader, Ernest Bevin. In telling the story of his life, Lucas has provided a fascinating range of insights into the lives of ordinary Londoners from the First World War until the outbreak of the Second World War. Threaded throughout is an account of such people's hunger for education, and of the different ways government, church and educational officialdom ministered to that hunger. *The Good That We Do* is both a study of one man and of a period when England changed, drastically and forever.
John Lucas is Professor of English at Nottingham Trent University and is a poet and critic.
2001 • 214 pages • ISBN 1-871551-54-4

In Pursuit of Lewis Carroll *by Raphael Shaberman*
Sherlock Holmes and the author uncover new evidence in their investigations into the mysterious life and writing of Lewis Carroll. They examine published works by Carroll that have been overlooked by previous commentators. A newly discovered poem, almost certainly by Carroll, is published here.
Amongst many aspects of Carroll's highly complex personality, this book explores his relationship with his parents, numerous child friends, and the formidable Mrs Liddell, mother of the immortal Alice. Raphael Shaberman was a founder member of the Lewis Carroll Society and a teacher of autistic children.
1994 • 118 pages • illustrated • ISBN 1-871551-13-7

Liar! Liar!: Jack Kerouac – Novelist *by R.J. Ellis*
The fullest study of Jack Kerouac's fiction to date. It is the first book to devote an individual chapter to every one of his novels. *On the Road*, *Visions of Cody* and *The Subterraneans* are reread in-depth, in a new and exciting way. *Visions of Gerard* and *Doctor Sax* are also strikingly reinterpreted, as are other daringly innovative writings, like 'The Railroad Earth' and his "try at a spontaneous *Finnegans Wake*" – *Old Angel Midnight*. Neglected writings, such as *Tristessa* and *Big Sur*, are also analysed, alongside better-known novels such as *Dharma Bums* and *Desolation Angels*.
R.J. Ellis is Senior Lecturer in English at Nottingham Trent University.
1999 • 295 pages • ISBN 1-871551-53-6

Musical Offering *by Yolanthe Leigh*

In a series of vivid sketches, anecdotes and reflections, Yolanthe Leigh tells the story of her growing up in the Poland of the 1930s and the Second World War. These are poignant episodes of a child's first encounters with both the enchantments and the cruelties of the world; and from a later time, stark memories of the brutality of the Nazi invasion, and the hardships of student life in Warsaw under the Occupation. But most of all this is a record of inward development; passages of remarkable intensity and simplicity describe the girl's response to religion, to music, and to her discovery of philosophy.

Yolanthe Leigh was formerly a Lecturer in Philosophy at Reading University.

2000 • 57 pages • ISBN: 1-871551-46-3

Norman Cameron *by Warren Hope*

Norman Cameron's poetry was admired by W.H. Auden, celebrated by Dylan Thomas and valued by Robert Graves. He was described by Martin Seymour-Smith as, "one of … the most rewarding and pure poets of his generation …" and is at last given a full length biography. This eminently sociable man, who had periods of darkness and despair, wrote little poetry by comparison with others of his time, but always of a consistently high quality – imaginative and profound.

2000 • 221 pages • illustrated • ISBN 1-871551-05-6

Poetry in Exile *by Michael Murphy*

"Michael Murphy discriminates the forms of exile and expatriation with the shrewdness of the cultural historian, the acuity of the literary critic, and the subtlety of a poet alert to the ways language and poetic form embody the precise contours of experience. His accounts of Auden, Brodsky and Szirtes not only cast much new light on the work of these complex and rewarding poets, but are themselves a pleasure to read." *Stan Smith, Research Professor in Literary Studies, Nottingham Trent University*

"In this brilliant book Murphy strives to get at the essence of 'poetry in exile' itself and to explain how it is at the centre of the whole political and cultural experience of the turbulent 20th century. His critical insight makes it one of the most important recent books on poetry in English." *Bernard O'Donoghue, Wadham College, Oxford*

Michael Murphy teaches English Literature at Liverpool Hope University College.

2004 • 268 pages • ISBN 1-871551-76-5

POETRY

Adam's Thoughts in Winter *by Warren Hope*
Warren Hope's poems have appeared from time to time in a number of literary periodicals, pamphlets and anthologies on both sides of the Atlantic. They appeal to lovers of poetry everywhere. His poems are brief, clear, frequently lyrical, characterised by wit, but often distinguished by tenderness. The poems gathered in this first book-length collection counter the brutalising ethos of contemporary life, speaking of and for the virtues of modesty, honesty and gentleness in an individual, memorable way.
2000 • 47 pages • ISBN 1-871551-40-4

Baudelaire: Les Fleurs du Mal *Translated by F.W. Leakey*
Selected poems from *Les Fleurs du Mal* are translated with parallel French texts and are designed to be read with pleasure by readers who have no French as well as those who are practised in the French language.
F.W. Leakey was Professor of French in the University of London. As a scholar, critic and teacher he specialised in the work of Baudelaire for 50 years and published a number of books on the poet.
2001 • 153 pages • ISBN 1-871551-10-2

'The Last Blackbird' and other poems by Ralph Hodgson *edited and introduced by John Harding*
Ralph Hodgson (1871-1962) was a poet and illustrator whose most influentialand enduring work appeared to great acclaim just prior to and during the First World War. His work is imbued with a spiritual passion for the beauty of creation and the mystery of existence. This new selection brings together, for the first time in 40 years, some of the most beautiful and powerful 'hymns to life' in the English language.
John Harding lives in London. He is a freelance writer and teacher and is Ralph Hodgson's biographer.
2004 • 70 pages • ISBN 1-871551-81-1

Lines from the Stone Age *by Sean Haldane*
Reviewing Sean Haldane's 1992 volume *Desire in Belfast*, Robert Nye wrote in *The Times* that "Haldane can be sure of his place among the English poets." This place is not yet a conspicuous one, mainly because his early volumes appeared in Canada and because he has earned his living by other means than literature. Despite this, his poems have always had their circle of readers. The 60 previously unpublished poems of *Lines from the Stone Age* – "lines of longing, terror, pride, lust and pain" – may widen this circle.
2000 • 53 pages • ISBN 1-871551-39-0

Shakespeare's Sonnets *by Martin Seymour-Smith*
Martin Seymour-Smith's outstanding achievement lies in the field of literary biography and criticism. In 1963 he produced his comprehensive edition, in the old spelling, of *Shakespeare's Sonnets* (here revised and corrected by himself and Peter Davies in 1998). With its landmark introduction and its brilliant critical commentary on each sonnet, it was praised by William Empson and John Dover Wilson. Stephen Spender said of him "I greatly admire Martin Seymour-Smith for the independence of his views and the great interest of his mind"; and both Robert Graves and Anthony Burgess described him as the leading critic of his time. His exegesis of the *Sonnets* remains unsurpassed.
2001 • 194 pages • ISBN 1-871551-38-2

Wilderness *by Martin Seymour-Smith*
This is Martin Seymour-Smith's first publication of his poetry for more than twenty years. This collection of 36 poems is a fearless account of an inner life of love, frustration, guilt, laughter and the celebration of others. He is best known to the general public as the author of the controversial and bestselling *Hardy* (1994).
1994 • 52 pages • ISBN 1-871551-08-0

BUSINESS

English Language Skills *by Vera Hughes*
If you want to be sure, (as a student, or in your business or personal life), that your written English is correct, this book is for you. Vera Hughes' aim is to help you remember the basic rules of spelling, grammar and punctuation. 'Noun', 'verb', 'subject', 'object' and 'adjective' are the only technical terms used. The book teaches the clear, accurate English required by the business and office world. It coaches acceptable current usage and makes the rules easier to remember.
Vera Hughes was a civil servant and is a trainer and author of training manuals.
2002 • 142 pages • ISBN 1-871551-60-9